THE PEASANT URBANITES

A Study of Rural-Urban Mobility in Serbia

This is the first volume in a series entitled

STUDIES IN ANTHROPOLOGY

Under the Consulting Editorship of E. A. Hammel, *University of California, Berkeley*

THE PEASANT URBANITES

A Study of Rural-Urban Mobility in Serbia

ANDREI ŠIMIĆ

Department of Sociology and Anthropology
University of Southern California
Los Angeles, California

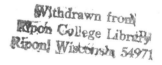

SEMINAR PRESS   1973   New York and London

SEMINAR PRESS, INC.
111 Fifth Avenue, New York, New York 10003

United Kingdom Edition published by
SEMINAR PRESS LIMITED
24/28 Oval Road, London NW1

LIBRARY OF CONGRESS CATALOG CARD NUMBER: 72-82125

PRINTED IN THE UNITED STATES OF AMERICA

To Jacque, Mark, and Saveta

CONTENTS

EDITOR'S PREFACE

Anthropological research has been characterized by a curious paradox—with its subject as Man, it has usually been pursued where there were rather few people. Some of it has been conjectural history, in which area there are no people at all, some has been honest history, in which the views of a few are taken to represent the many, and most of the rest has been concerned with a state of existence in which very few men have ever lived since the beginning of time. The last thirty-odd years have seen a change, of course, first with the growing interest in peasants (as the next-best thing to real savages), but more recently there has been an explicit concern with urban man.

This concern, it seems to me, is motivated by pressing interests and is long overdue. The anthropologist of urban life does not seek to find the nature of Man by looking at his naked brethren but rather by observing Man in that state in which he lives. Furthermore, he is brought to his subject not by romantic or conjectural interests but by pressing need. It is in the cities of the world that the drama of human life is now played, and it is in the cities that the foundation is being laid for the future of us all. Most of the action is occurring in the so-called developing nations, those nations but recently freed from the colonial yoke, where most of the population of the world lives. These new nations are now experiencing on a drastically foreshortened time scale the events that overtook Western Europe and North America a century and more ago.

Yugoslavia is of particular interest among these nations, since like so many others, it is made up of the remnants of more than one decayed empire, beset by internal ethnic differences, and struggling to find internal peace and international security at the same time. Again, like others, the Yugoslav state is Marxian Socialist in ideology and the product of a successful peasant rebellion. It has come to have that blend of proudly sensitive nationalism, anti-colonialism, collectivism, and a driving urge to modernize and industrialize which we now recognize as typical of such developing nation-states. Some showed these features in pre-Leninist times, like Mexico and Turkey, others afterward, like China, Cuba, and Algeria. For the anthropologist, who has been fortunate to be able to work in Yugoslavia as he frequently may not in other such countries, it provides the opportunity to understand the effects of the currents of history on the lives of ordinary men—in brief, a proper subject for the anthropologist to observe and study.

Professor Simić brings to his task a childhood bilingualism capped by later acquired skills as a polyglot and a lifetime of participant observation in the culture of his Serbian forebears, on both sides of the Atlantic. Like Admic's, his is a tale of a native's return. He was rightly accepted by his hosts as one of their own, in a way that few if any foreign ethnographers have ever been, and his participation in everyday life was thorough and intimate, from the schooling of his children to the hospitalization of his wife, ranging from serious academic discussion in the institutes to drunken raillery in the *kafanas*. Professor Simić has drawn for us a very close sketch of what happens to man when he is moved wholesale from his peasant origins to the clank and grind of city life, when his political and economic world is turned upside down. This is a fine appreciation of the bases of man's decisions, of his fundamental rationality, and of the sources of stability he finds in a sea of change.

E. A. HAMMEL
Berkeley

ACKNOWLEDGMENTS

Field work is fundamental to anthropological research. It provides the basic materials of the discipline without which a study such as this would be impossible. Thus, I would like to express a debt of gratitude to those institutions which enabled me to carry out research on three occasions in Yugoslavia. During the summer of 1966 a 3-month stay in Belgrade and the village of Borina in Western Serbia was financed by a Training Grant from the National Institutes of Health (National Institute of General Medical Sciences, Grant No. GM-1224). It was during this period that the basic plan of this study was formulated. The body of data was collected during a year's residence in Belgrade (March 1968–March 1969) financed by grants from the National Institutes of Health (Grant No. GM-1224), and the Center for Slavic and East European Studies and the Department of Anthropology at the University of California at Berkeley. During the summer of 1970 further field work was carried out in four villages which had contributed respondents to the Belgrade sample and material previously gathered in the Yugoslav capital was updated. This trip was made possible by grants from the Wenner-Gren Foundation for Anthropological Research and the American Philosophical Society.

I would like to express a particular debt to Professor Eugene A. Hammel for his constant encouragement and advice as well as for his sincere interest in my work. I would also like to thank Professors May N. Diaz and Wolfram Eberhard for their criticisms and useful observations regarding this study. The sympathetic cooperation of numerous Yugoslav friends and colleagues was indispensable to the successful completion of this research. I would especially like to thank Dr. Anton Vratuša, former Yugoslav Ambassador to the United Nations, for his invaluable aid in facilitating the carrying out of field work in Yugoslavia. I am also greatly indebted to the Institute of Social Sciences in Belgrade under whose auspices the research was conducted. I would particularly like to mention and thank Dr. Ilija Stanojčić, Dr. Firdus Džinić, Dr. Olivera Burić, Danica Kurtović, and Radiša Despotović. I am grateful to Radomir Antić and Nevenka Rodić of the Rad Construction Enterprise for their help in establishing contact with a number of their workers. For their valuable observations regarding Serbian urbanization I would like to express my appreciation to Dr. Dragomir Davidović and Jelena Špadijer-Džinić of the Institute for Criminological and Criminalistic Research, and Dr. Ninko Samardžija of the Secretariat for Internal Affairs in Belgrade. I would also like to give special thanks to my friend, Vladan Marković, for his aid in establishing contact with many of the informants who participated in the study, and for our many insightful conversations.

Finally, there is no way I can adequately express my appreciation to my wife for the many hours of work she contributed typing field notes and editing manuscripts. She willingly and unselfishly gave of both her time and energy.

GUIDE TO PRONUNCIATION
OF SERBO-CROATIAN

č ch as in the English *chant*

ć palatalized č, similar to the t in the English *pasture*

c ts as in the English *cats*

dž j as in the English *jam*

dj palatalized dž, similar to the elision of d and y in the English *bad year*

j y as in the English *yes*

lj li as in the English *million*

nj ny as in the English *canyon*

r rolled as in Spanish, appears also as a vowel (vocalic r) with a pronunciation somewhat similar to er in the English *pert* š   sh as in the English *shape*

ž   z as in the English *azure*

Other vowels and consonants are pronounced approximately as in Spanish. Stress tends to fall on the first syllable, and stressed and unstressed vowels receive their full value. Serbo-Croatian and Slovene are distinguished from other Slavic languages by their system of long and short vowels and tonal accent whose qualities cannot be adequately described here.

CHAPTER I

INTRODUCTION

Social anthropologists, who formerly limited their research to the study of small, relatively homogenous nonindustrial cultures, have during the past several decades shifted their attention to the problems of complex societies, and in particular to the analysis of questions related to urbanism, urbanization, and social and cultural change under the impact of modernization. There are three essential ways in which they have viewed the city. Urban centers have been considered as a focus of political and economic power, and as agents of change for the hinterland. A second approach has documented the growth and development of the city through the incorporation of peasant and tribal migrants. A third perspective has centered on the life of the city per se, usually delineating limited problems or singling out small, easily defined groups within the population that are amenable to traditional ethnological methodology. Though all three of these viewpoints are implicit in this work, it is to the second that I shall direct my principal interest.

A major theme of the twentieth century has been the metamorphosis of tribal peoples and subsistence agriculturalists into an urban proletariat. As Foster has noted (1967a, p. 7), the contemporary city and the superstates that follow in its wake do not produce peasants. Regarding this, Potter (1967a) views the comparative study of the modernization process as it relates to the world's peasantries as "one of the most important areas in anthropological research [p. 378]." Indeed, in many parts of the world, as in northwestern Europe, peasants have all but disappeared, whereas in other areas they still constitute the dominant societal type or linger on, providing a pool of reserve labor for industrializing states. It is in such so-called *developing nations* that the social scientist is provided with a living laboratory for the study of the dynamics of modernization and urbanization, a salient feature of which is the massive migration of rural peoples to the city and their subsequent acculturation to contemporary urban life.

In 1940, Henrick Van Loon predicted that Serbia could not look forward to a great future as an industrial state. In his encapsulated minigeography of the world, in which he devoted three pages to Yugoslavia, he made the observation that "Belgrade may forever remain an amiable little country town [p. 272]." In conclusion, however, he qualified these statements with a remark which later proved to be, at least in part, accurate: "The Serbian peasant would not be the first to have his sound ancestral standards upset by the counterfeit cultural ideal of our Hollywood prophets [p. 272]." Of course, at that time, few could have foreseen the extent of the changes which were to sweep the technologically underdeveloped areas of the globe following the close of the Second World War.

The headlong rush of the Yugoslavs into the twentieth century has not been an isolated phenomenon, but one which has typified the recent history of many former colonial and preindustrial peoples. Though the goals of modernization and the resultant emerging *world culture* may seem alarmingly uniform, it is my belief that the experience of each people will reflect their own specific historical and cultural context. It is with this assumption that I propose to examine urbanization as a facet of the recent transformation of Yugoslav life.

Evans-Pritchard (1962) has pointed out that "a people's traditional history is important for the . . . reason that it forms part of the thought of living man and hence part of the social life which the anthropologist can directly observe [p. 51]." In this respect, Yugoslavia provides a setting unlike any other in Europe. Though the Balkan Slavs share many characteristics in common with their Mediterranean neighbors,[1] they are in many respects unique, a circumstance attributable in part to their centuries-long marginality to the major philosophical, political, and cultural currents of Europe and the Middle East. During the height of Greco–Roman civilization, the Slavs had not yet penetrated beyond the Danube into the Balkan Peninsula. Their migration southward into the Thraco–Illyrian lands and the Pelopponesus in the seventh century brought them to the fringes of Byzantium. Though the Serbs and Bulgars accepted Christianity, the alphabet, and other elements of Hellenic culture from the Greeks, they were to remain peripheral to the Empire, a partially assimilated and often troublesome people for the Byzantines. With the subjugation of the Balkans by the Turks in the fourteenth and fifteenth centuries, though many were Islamized, the Balkan Slavs continued to live for the most part, as tribalists, or became peasant serfs of the Ottomans without effective participation in the sophisticated great tradition of the cities. On the other hand, the fate of the Croats and Slovenes was tied to that of the Franks and later the Austro-Hungarians. They occupied a somewhat remote and primitive appendage of Central Europe, standing as a buffer between the Hapsburgs and the Turks. During the nineteenth century the influence of European nationalism was felt in the Balkans and the awakened aspirations culminated in the creation of a South Slav state following the First World War. However, the new Yugoslavia remained industrially dependent on the Western nations, who looked to the Balkans as a source of raw materials and agricultural produce. In the years following the Second World War, Yugoslavia found

---

[1]The Mediterranean has frequently been regarded as a single-culture area (cf. Peristiany, 1965; Pitt-Rivers, 1963). To cite one example, attitudes in the Balkans regarding sex-role behavior are very similar to those prevalent in other parts of southern Eurpoe and the Middle East (Hammel, 1967; Simić,1969).

herself balancing between East and West, isolated from the main-stream of world Marxism, pursuing an "independent road to socialism." The contemporary Yugoslavs do, however, share with other emerging nations the determination to participate fully in modern life through the development of an industrial base. In this goal they have achieved considerable success, as is attested to by the country's rapid economic growth over the past 25 years and the concomitant appearance of a cadre of highly trained pro-fessionals, skilled workers, and technicians. New productive capacities and work positions have made possible the influx of large numbers of villagers to Yugoslavia's rapidly expanding urban centers.

I propose to view Yugoslav urbanization from several perspec-tives: in a comparative frame of reference as part of a worldwide trend; as the specific product of its own historical and cultural context; and finally, in its dynamic dimensions as reflected by case studies collected during a year's field work in Belgrade. Though I regard the experience of the individual actor as my primary focus, the data suggest that no single analytic perspective is adequate to the task. For example, the structural and functional approach that has been applied so frequently in the past by anthropologists to the study of small, relatively homogeneous folk societies has considerable utility in the interpretation of traditional village social organization, the understanding of which is essential to the analysis of culture change in Serbia. On the other hand, research in complex societies has prompted the development of new conceptual and methodological tools focusing on social pro-cess rather than the creation of static models based on group interaction within an institutional framework. Illustrative of this is the fact that urban life, with its more amorphous and fluid pattern of social relationships, generally lends itself less to the formulation of normative rules than to description in terms of observed regularities and spectrums of behavior. In this regard an important theoretical trend has been one in which social rela-tionships have been metaphorically and analytically likened to a network in which some, but not all, of the component units maintain ties with each other (Barnes, 1954, 1968; Bott, 1955, 1957; Mitchell, 1969). Such a model conforms to the increased individuality evident in the acculturation to urban life, and indeed, the importance of individual choice and selectivity within historically and culturally determined limits (cf. Foster, 1961, 1963) must be recognized as a salient aspect of the migratory and urbanization process.

It is my intention to view rural–urban mobility in its broadest sense, not only in terms of its initial phases as an act of spatial relocation, but also as a continuing process of social and cultural adjustment after settlement in the city. My approach will be topical, following the migrant through the various stages of his transformation from peasant to urbanite. Among problems I will consider are the nature and variety of stimuli for migration; physical and economic adaptation to city life; the role of traditional values and ideology as reflected in rural–urban reciprocity; the creation of urban social networks; and the manner in which individuals perceive the urbanization experience and their new environment.

Lipset and Bendix (1963) have noted that "widespread social mobility has been a concomitant of industrialization and a basic characteristic of modern industrial society [p.11]." Though a great deal is known about the historic, economic, and political development of the modern industrial state, very little is yet understood regarding this process as a social and personal phenomenon. Similarly, there has been a paucity of anthropological data regarding the Balkans. For example, prior to the Second World War, research in Yugoslavia had been limited, for the most part, to the work of native ethnographers, who were generally guided by fairly narrow nationalistic concerns.[2] During the last twenty years, however, there has been a growing interest in Yugoslavia, which until recently was the only Eastern European socialist state in which foreign scholars were relatively free to carry out independent research. Moreover, the country's rapid industrialization and the emergence of so-called *national communism*, with its accompanying democratization, economic decentralization, and system of workers' self-management, have aroused considerable academic interest in the West. It is hoped that this investigation of the personal consequences of rural–urban migration and urbanization will contribute to our knowledge of social mobility and modernization in developing nations, and add new dimensions to the expanding anthropological literature on the Balkans.

[2]Regarding the history and characteristics of the social sciences in Yugoslavia, see Halpern and Hammel (1969).

CHAPTER II

INDUSTRIALIZATION AND SOCIOCULTURAL CHANGE

Introduction

Urban living is not a new phenomenon, and cities as foci for government, commerce, the arts, crafts, intellectual life, and ritual have existed since the Neolithic period.[1] For thousands of years, the form and function of the city had remained more or less static, in a relationship of mutual dependence with the majority of the population, who were rural agriculturalists. All this was to be changed, however, by the industrialism that sprang up in Western Europe and America during the nineteenth and twentieth centuries. The ensuing technological revolution not only

---

[1]Regarding the origins of urban life, see Adams (1966), Childe (1964), Davis (1955), Frankfort (1956), Glyn (1968), Hawkes and Woolley (1963), and Sanders and Price (1968), among others.

6

stimulated the growth of urban centers, but also altered the very structure and quality of society.

These transformations are perhaps most clearly reflected in the metamorphosis of urban life, an interpretation of which depends on an understanding of its traditional form and antecedents. The contemporary city is the culmination of a process of growth and diversification of an earlier urban type which, though occasionally large, socially and culturally more closely resembled a village than it did its modern counterpart. The nature and function of the *preindustrial city* have been extensively delineated by Sjoberg (1960), and even today many contemporary urban complexes still conform in varying degrees to this pattern. In terms of population and spatial dimensions it was small,[2] and characterized by congestion and crowding. Narrow and often tortuous streets inhibited rapid internal communication and the flow of goods. It was frequently divided into self-sufficient ethnic or occupational quarters. Religious edifices and the homes of the elite formed the nucleus, with the lower strata of the populace relegated to the outskirts. Water and sewage systems were generally inadequate, and sanitation so poor that epidemics were a constant threat. Social relationships were conducted on the basis of personalistic standards, and status was ascribed by birth and position in a kinship network. Marriage was the rule, and it bound families, not individuals. Large extended households were common, and there was little or no generational conflict. Economic and social individualism was severely limited. Commerce and industry were characterized by a low level of technology, and mass production for the market was absent. The use of time was capricious, and negative attitudes toward work prevailed. Government was validated by tradition or through an appeal to absolutes. Power struggles among the elite were common, and church and state tended to be inseparable. Such a society severely restricted personal mobility because of the lack of universal criteria for judging men and their products, and the standard of living remained, for most, at a subsistence plane due to an underdeveloped technology and the absence of a work ethic.

[2]Sirjamaki (1964, pp. 79–80), for example, estimates the thirteenth–century populations of Venice, Florence, and Milan at approximately 100,000 inhabitants each. Of Western Europe's population of 60,000,000 persons in the second quarter of the fourteenth century, about 10% lived in urban settlements.

Sjoberg's principal hypothesis is that the form and structure of preindustrial cities everywhere more closely resemble one another than they do the modern industrial urban center. He distinguishes three general types of society: the *folk*, or *preliterate*; the *feudal preindustrial*; and the *industrial-urban* variant. Technology is the key independent variable in formulating this typology. The folk society has no cities, its technology is rudimentary, and most of the populace's time is devoted to food gathering. Feudal society has more advanced agriculture, surpluses to support a nonagricultural population, a fairly simple technology, and animate sources of power. It possesses cities of the preindustrial type, but most of the population is agrarian. The industrial–urban society depends on inanimate energy sources, "science" is important; a large percentage of the population lives in cities; the class system is fluid; achievement is more common than ascription; social power is diffused; the conjugal family is the ideal norm, with kinship playing a relatively minor role in human relations. The modern economic system is rationalized, is characterized by a greater division of labor, and is highly standardized. Norms tend to be permissive and idiosyncratic, and there is widespread literacy. (For further elaboration, see Sjoberg, 1960, pp. 4–12.)

Clearly the three societal types formulated by Sjoberg coexist in the contemporary world, and "development" has generally been taken to mean change in the direction of what he terms industrial-urban society. This type of community has grown up as the result of industrialization with its increased productive capacity and the associated proliferation of technology. This phenomenon has centered principally in Western Europe, North America, and their extensions. Thus, such terms as *modernization, westernization, world culture, developed*, and *developing* bear a direct relationship and correspondence to the culture, economics, and institutions of the more industrialized nations of the world. Inversely, *primitive, underdeveloped, traditional*, and *backward* refer to folk and feudal societies. Though these terms remain defined in only the broadest manner, and are the product of a kind of general understanding and consensus rather than a precise set of delineated meanings, their value as a descriptive and classificatory device remains clear despite the diffuseness of their application. It is in the context of their most generalized definitions that this terminology will be employed throughout this work.

Social and cultural characteristics of the modern Western community have been diffused throughout the traditional world as a result of colonialism and the more recent emergence of political and economic nationalism. In former colonial regions, cities on a European plan had proliferated as externally imposed commercial and administrative centers. In other areas, political and economic revolution and reform, coupled with increased productive capacities and technological advancement, have transformed urban life, drawing on a Western model. The metamorphosis of many traditional societies during the decades since the close of the Second World War has been accelerated not only by the ideology of national independence, but also by the belief that through industrialization it is possible to join the ranks of the powerful and prosperous.

Anderson (1964) comments that "a country with a high level of industrialism also possesses a high level of urbanism [p. 1]." However, industry alters not only the scale of the city, but also its function and cultural content. The countryside is likewise transformed, since subsistence cultivation and primitive hunting and gathering are not generally concomitants of the industrial–urban complex. Contemporary economies encourage farming for profit and reinvestment, thereby converting the peasantry into rural entrepreneurs or, in other cases (e.g., under some Marxist regimes), into an agricultural proletariat (cf. Potter, 1967b; Halpern, 1967).

The increase in the size of cities and the proliferation of urban communities have been worldwide phenomena; however, in terms of the rapidity of social and cultural change, the implications for contemporary non-Western peoples have been most profound. For traditional societies modernization signifies not merely an inrease in magnitude, but also a change in the very nature of human relationships. For the individual, urbanization involves not only moving to a city, and a concomitant reorientation from agricultural to other pursuits, but also a shift in patterns of behavior and belief. Adjustment to a new sociocultural context and the acquiring of control over an unfamiliar environment frequently require the abandonment of traditional customs and values. It has become increasingly evident, however, that urbanization and modernization are not a single process, but that they exhibit considerable cross-cultural variation. Economic development may occur in such a way that changes are incorporated and absorbed into the indigenous social and cultural structure, whereas in other cases, modern elements may coexist with traditional features without integration. On the other hand, the pressures of modernization may totally destroy preindustrial life styles, often bringing about psychological and social disintegration of peoples unable to come to terms with new conditions of life (cf. the *Antlers*, Mead, 1932). In this regard, it should be noted that modern society developed slowly over several centuries in the West, permitting a gradual accommodation to the needs of an expanding industrial–urban economy. Contemporary Westerners are accustomed to a culture in which the individual habitually faces a number of alternatives for behavioral response to given situations.

The Intermediate Society

In nations where change has come about very rapidly, one often finds a community in which traditional and modern elements coexist, frequently in sharp contrast or conflict with each other. These societies can be regarded as *intermediate* in that they are no longer totally *traditional*, but have yet to complete the transformation into modern industrial states. In such cases, and these perhaps represent the most widespread societal type in the contemporary world, one finds two cultural systems operating simultaneously, sometimes in harmony and mutual dependence, and sometimes in opposition, inhibiting development.

Although nations occupying intermediate positions in terms of industrial development and levels of modernization and urbanization will show considerable individual variation, according to their particular historical, cultural, and social context, they appear to share sufficient similarities to enable us to make some general statements regarding them.

An intermediate society will have experienced, or will be in the process of undergoing, a national revival, with its implications for cultural and political autonomy. Innovations will be initiated by or transmitted through, the medium of a national political entity. Mills (1961), for example, regards the *nation-state* as the natural framework for the formulation of modern social problems:

The nation-state is now the dominating form in world history and, as such, a major fact in the life of every man. The nation-state has split up and organized, in varying degree and manner, the "civilizations" and continents of the world. The extent of its spread and the stages of its development are major clues to modern and now to world history. Within the nation-state, the political and military, cultural and economic means of decision and power are now organized; all the institutions and specific milieux in which most men live their public and private lives are now organized into one or the other of the nation-states.[3]

Within the developing nation, innovation will center in the large cities, which act as points of diffusion to the countryside.[4] In many cases there will be only one urban complex of any size, usually the capital city.[5] The major population centers, which contain the locus of economic and political power as well as a nation's intellectual elite, are a logical starting point for the study of modernization. Cities are the most frequent funnels for foreign goods, ideas, and influence, and are foci upon which lines of communication from the outside world converge. The city is the meeting place for diverse cultural elements, and acts as a leveling device, integrating disparate factions and groups into a new super-regional whole. Urban complexes thus serve as the nuclei for the formation of national tradition.[6]

[3]From C. W. Mills, *The Sociological Imagination*, page 135. Grove Press, New York, 1961. Copyright 1959 by Oxford Univ. Press, London and New York.

[4]Foster (1962, p. 29) explains the role of the city as an agent of change in terms of the prestige associated with urban areas. Change has customarily been initiated among the upper classes and then spread downward to the traditionally inarticulate lower classes, and finally outward to the countryside.

[5]Such a city is commonly referred to as a *primate city*. Latin America, for instance, shows a high primacy pattern in urban growth. Mexico is a case in point, with Mexico City containing seven times the population of Guadalajara, the second largest metropolitan center. In 16 out of 21 Latin American countries the first city is at least 3.7 times larger than the second city (Browning, 1968, pp. Bog-4a). For further comments regarding the primate city, see Breese (1966, pp. 48-49).

[6]In his study of migrants in Mexico City, Butterworth (1962) makes the following observations regarding the Mixtec Indian subjects of his research. "Many of the residents of Mexico City display an increased awareness of and identification with the Mexican nation [p. 265]."

In many parts of the former colonial world nation-states are just emerging in an incipient form. These may be regarded as essentially prenational, while in other areas former national states have been combined into larger political entities (i.e., the Soviet Union, Yugoslavia) and must again experience the process of integration of dissimilar and often opposing regional units.

Most intermediate societies contain traditional cities, which, due to industrialization, are experiencing an exceedingly rapid growth of population without an equivalent expansion of facilities, housing, and services, and in many cases the appearance of vast slums or squatter settlements is a concomitant of urbanization.[7] City life does not necessarily bring about an improvement in the migrant's standard of living, and Breese (1966, p. 5) describes what he terms *subsistence urbanization*, a concept borrowed from the idea of *subsistence agriculture*. This corresponds to an urban situation in which people have only the bare necessities of life, and Breese indicates that the majority of citizens in newly developing countries live under such conditions. These circumstances are associated with a rate of urbanization which often exceeds that of industrial growth, and a low level of productivity per individual worker.

A significant percentage of the urban population in transitional societies consists of recent arrivals from the village or tribe. Moreover, many workers in the city are in fact commuting, part-time agriculturalists or seasonal laborers tied as closely to the countryside as to the city.[8] Thus, the urban community, while an agent for the diffusion of modern culture, also experiences peasantization,[9] since rural folkways are brought into the city as part of the baggage of migrants.[10] In developing nations there is frequently a striking similarity between the city working classes and their rural counterparts.[11] For instance, attitudes developed in agricultural life are often brought over into urban activities. Time, for example, may not be fully regarded as a commodity, and daily regularity of schedule and punctuality therefore remain alien concepts.

[7]Regarding the formation of squatter settlements and their characteristics see, among others, Bonilla (1970), Mangin (1967, 1970b–d), and Turner (1970).

[8]For examples from the Soviet Union, see Halpern (1967, pp. 104–106) and from Yugoslavia, Kostić (1955). Also, refer to Breese (1966, pp. 84–85) regarding seasonal

In the intermediate society there is a significantly wider cultural gap between the educated elite and lower classes than in contemporary Western countries. Rural migrants often remain alienated from urban institutions outside the scope of their immediate economic interests, and fail to fully utilize public facilities, such as banks, schools, and public health centers. They do not feel entirely at home in the city, and this insecurity is liable to be expressed in the form of anxiety or ambivalence regarding urban custom. On the other hand, strong lines of economic, social, and ritual reciprocity are frequently maintained with rural kin, and in some cases geographical mobility may be inhibited by kinship obligations or regional attachments.

Urban centers in developing nations still evidence many characteristics of the traditional, preindustrial city. Small independent craftsmen carry on their work in cramped quarters under primitive conditions, utilizing a backward technology. Door-to-door and street merchants, dealing in small quantities of goods, are common, and there is frequent direct exchange between producer and consumer. The majority of the populace still obtains its food through a system of peasant marketing. Physically, the

---

and temporary migration, and Moore (1965, pp. 76–80) for a general discussion of migration as a consequence of economic development.

[9]Abu-Lugod (1961) provides an example from Egypt.

[10]Kostić (1969) comments regarding this phenomenon in Yugoslav cities:

> The process of migration and settlement of peasants is a continuing phenomenon, and has very significant consequences for both the peasants and the society of the cities in which they have settled 'peasantized.' ... The new population has its particular cultural needs, and this is especially evident in relation to so-called mass culture in that the press, radio, television and other means of mass communication must take cognizance of their presence and numbers.

[11]Lewis (1952) noted the similarity between many aspects of life in Mexico City and that in Tepoztlán, and concluded that the essentially traditional nature of the capital city was conducive to a satisfactory adjustment of peasant migrants. In this regard, Foster (1953a, pp. 169–170) comments that large segments of Latin American urban populations are more typically folk than anything else, and the presence or absence of folk culture in cities and towns seems to be a function of the particular type of urban center involved. Despite the recent industialization which has characterized many Latin American cities, in social form they have remained essentially preindustrial. As examples he cites family organization, the status of women, employer–worker relationships, formal and informal mechanisms for maintaining law and order, and attitudes toward religion. Foster believes that there is an inevitable lag between rapidly changing manufacturing and marketing techniques, and less flexible traditional sociocultural forms which are increasingly unsuited to the needs of modern economies.

"animal-drawn vehicles share the streets with automobiles . . ." Belgrade outskirts

city projects an image of striking contrast, with high-rise apartments looming above adobe hovels and collapsing ancient buildings. Traditional and modern dress are evident in city crowds, and animal-drawn vehicles share the streets with automobiles and trucks.[12] Whereas the central district may appear totally modern, with wide asphalt boulevards, department stores, and imposng edifices of government and commerce, the outskirts resemble a village, with narrow alleyways of cobblestone or earth. Here residents continue to engage in agricultural practices, such as the keeping of kitchen gardens and the raising of livestock and fowl.

Finally, the city in many modernizing countries is a showplace and not necessarily indicative of the general level of development in the nation. Resources are frequently invested in the construction of expensive and nonproductive monuments which symbolize the society's emergence from *primitivism* and the role of the government and its leaders in this process.

[12]Breese (1965) cites the following example from India. The transportation "mix" in large Indian urban areas further complicates circulation. . . . Animal and vehicular transportation ranges from sluggish camel and donkey to the speeding truck and rapid commuter train. [From Gerald Breese, *Urbanization in Newly Developing Countries*, pages 56–57. Copyright ☉ 1966, Prentice-Hall, Inc., Englewood Cliffs, New Jersey.].

While a significant percentage of the nation's population still remains in rural villages, lines of communication with the city are noticeably more efficient than in the preindustrial period, and there is an increasing dependence on modern technology in the countryside. Thus, the disparity between urban and rural life styles is continually diminishing,[13] there is greater homogeneity of national life, and regional variation in language, culture, and sentiment becomes less pronounced.

In conclusion, it should be emphasized that the intermediate society is best analyzed, not in terms of a static structural model, but in its dynamic dimensions. Anthropologists have long recognized that no society exists in a perfect state of equilibrium, and that change is an essential characteristic of human social organization; in many tribal and traditional peasant communities, however, the rate of change is sufficiently slow so as to allow a greater analytical emphasis on continuing organizational principles. On the other hand, European and American industrial culture is not only more complex, but also in a state of constant and rapid flux. Bohannan (1963) has suggested that the accommodation to Western culture is not "merely adjusting to a single and stable new situation: one must adjust to adjusting [p. 387]."

Urbanization and Modernization:
The Individual as the Locus of Change

To date, most of our knowledge and documentation of the process of modernization, industrialization, and urbanization in primitive and traditional societies has been gained from the viewpoint of the major formal economic and political institutions of the nation, while rural–urban migration has been described mostly in terms of its gross demographic features and in the light of historic causality. In contrast to this approach, anthropologists have generally attempted to portray the community as a whole, usually working in small, relatively simple social entities in tribal

---

[13]Halpern (1967) states, regarding the modernization of the countryside, that "one of the characteristics of the modern political state appears to be the attempt to eliminate the distinctions between urban and rural life." [From Joel M. Halpern, *The Changing Village Community*, page 2. Copyright © 1967, Prentice Hall, Inc., Englewood Cliffs, New Jersey.]

or peasant societies, where the instruments of politics, religion, and economics are most often a function of the family, kinship, sex, and age. Since in such societies there is usually little or no distinction between formal and informal levels of organization, and specialization of labor and knowledge is limited, each man is able to participate more directly in the totality of social and cultural life. Thus, to a great extent, all men share more or less the same assumptions and expectations, and an understanding of the role of the individual is implicit in the nature of the culture. This does not hold true in the modern industrial community, and though change is ultimately explicable by the decisions and actions of individuals, the personal consequences of national trends cannot be inferred from the general characteristics of the society. [14] With this in mind, and without abandoning the traditional methodology and focus of the anthropologist, the question of contemporary industrial development in Yugoslavia, and its cultural repercussions will be approached in this work from the perspective of the individual as both an interpreter and an agent of change.

Denitch (1969, pp. 3–7), in her study of a growing industrial town in Serbia, stresses that the large-scale social mobility which has taken place in Yugoslavia since the close of the Second World War is primarily the result of voluntary action on the part of individuals who made decisions regarding the favorability of leaving traditional villages to pursue life in urban centers. She assumes that certain kinds of behavior are based on conscious choices made from among alternatives perceived to exist in a given situation. On the other hand, it should be noted that general social, political,

---

[14]The opposition between simple and complex societies has been frequently described in terms of contrasting principles of social integration. Tönnies (1957), for example formulated the dichotomy between *Gemeinschaft* (community) and *Gesellschaft* (society), the former characterized by a social cohesion based on intimate personal relationships, and the latter by conscious social contract. Similarly, Durkheim (1964) differentiated between societal types in terms of *mechanical* and *organic solidarity*. Mechanical solidarity applies to simple societies with a minimal division of labor and a "collective conscience," whereas organic solidarity corresponds to complex societies characterized by a complementary division of labor and the lack of a single body of social interest. These models were further elaborated by Redfield and articulated in his formulation of the *folk–urban continuum,* a model derived in part from field materials gathered in Yucatán (1941), and which provided the basis of much of his subsequent work (1947, 1950, 1953, 1955, 1956a, b).

and economic conditions will restrict the range of possible courses of action.[15] Within such limits, however, questions may be posed regarding variables related to the decision-making process and the hierarchy of priorities brought to bear in the consideration of possible alternatives for strategic action.

Breese (1966, pp. 80–82) points out that in developing countries migration to the city is the result of both the "pull" of urban life and the "push" of existing rural circumstances. Diverse motivations interact in the life histories of migrants, and single variables are seldom determinants of important choices that alter the normal life expectations of individuals. For example, he cites as motivative factors in emigration: rural overpopulation, with its accompanying shortage of workable land; the lack of nonagricultural employment opportunities in the countryside; and the problem of seasonal inactivity or unemployment on the part of agriculturalists. The city, on the other hand, gives promise of increased economic opportunity, access to education, better facilities, greater variety, and freedom from the traditional restraints of village life.

Max Weber, in his study of German agrarian society at the close of the nineteenth century, was able to relate migration from eastern Germany to fluctuations in the world market. However, on a more specific level, he found that individual motivations played an important role. He concluded that rational economic interests were secondary to ideological considerations. Many of the best workers on annual contract with ample earnings chose migration rather than to remain in a subservient position. Weber believed that this stemmed from a psychological fascination with freedom, a basic drive which superseded material and economic considerations.[16] From this it can be implied that, given the economic feasibility of migration from an individual's place of

---

[15] In this regard Denitch cites Barth (1963):
The view we adopt is that all social activity may be analyzed as a result of constrained choices, and thereby connected with the variables of "value" and "purpose." Statistical regularities or patterns in the behavior of a population, as well as institutionalized patterns (i.e., the general acceptance of the expected patterns), may be expected to result where a set of external factors limit choice and in conjunction with a certain set of evaluations define clear strategic optima [p. 7].

[16] See Bendix (1962) for a discussion and analysis of Weber's work *Die Verhältnisse der Landarbeiter im ostelbischen Deutschland* (1892).

origin, nonmaterial factors will significantly influence the decision-making process. Thus, the interpretation of the process of urbanization and modernization depends, to an equal degree, on an understanding of its cultural roots and ramifications, as well as its political and economic foundations.

A summary of several points made earlier will serve to place the question of the role of culture in the transformation of the contemporary world in its proper perspective. Folk and urban culture have been commonly regarded as reflecting two opposing societal types. The former has been characterized by homogeneity, a high level of integration of the component institutions, and a consensus as to values and behavioral expectations. The city, on the other hand, is ostensibly heterogeneous in its makeup, offering greater anonymity, and a wider repertoire of sanctioned behavioral alternatives. It has been demonstrated, however, that the preindustrial city in many ways does not conform to this stereotype, and that urban life in developing nations evidences many characteristics associated with so-called *folk cultures*. The folk–urban dichotomy is therefore better applied in distinguishing modern industrial societies from traditional ones, and in the case of *intermediate societies* we can expect to find a synthesis of the two divergent cultural systems, or elements of both coexisting side by side.

Problems of adaptation to industrial life must be faced, not only by rural migrants, but also by the more traditional strata of urban populations in developing nations. The degree of involvement in contemporary society is at least initially limited both by the ability of the individual to perceive and manipulate new symbols and by his desire to do so. The transitional period can be characterized as a situation in which a person must learn to function in terms of several cultural systems simultaneously. It would appear that the internalization of contrasting norms and expectations can be accomplished without undue stress if these are not mutually exclusive or excessively conflicting in their demands. For instance, it will be shown that traditional corporate kinship obligations can be honored at the same time that new and more individualistic networks of social interaction are being cultivated in terms of values related to personal mobility.

Hammel (1964) has described culture in its relationship to society as an information system containing a series of messages regarding statuses. This concept can provide a useful analytical device for the interpretation of the process of transformation from a simple to a more complex social environment. He states:

> The more complex a society is in its structure of statuses, the more complex must be its cultural code for the transmission of status identification betwen actors. If manipulation of statuses is important (and I believe it always is), the cultural code must always be a little more complex than the series of messages it is to transmit; it must have a degree of entropy sufficient to allow both ambiguity and redundancy [p. 85].

In terms of this theory most traditional societies may be typified as possessing relatively few statuses differentiated by a small number of culturally determined criteria. Hammel has indicated that such cultures exhibit a low level of ambiguity, and comprise information systems of "low entropy" with a high level of internal organization. In contrast, urbanization and industrialization are associated with an increasing complexity of social organization characterized by more intricate and less homogeneous cultural guidelines.

Accommodation to contemporary urban culture involves the internalization of new, more involute and equivocal criteria by which to judge men and their behavior. Moreover, in a rapidly changing heterogeneous milieu we seldom find the consensus common to small traditional communities, where there is a high degree of unanimity regarding the basis by which people and their actions shall be evaluated. In the modern city the weight of judgment rests to a greater extent with the individual, who must often consciously measure conflicting, and frequently ill-perceived, evidence regarding the motives and identity of those with whom he must deal.

Industrial growth and economic expansion not only bring about the creation of a greater number of new work positions, but also make it possible for more individuals to progress upward through a hierarchy of statuses, since there is more room at the top (see Hammel, 1969b, p. 54). In this way development sets the stage for both horizontal and vertical mobility. Addressing his attention to the cultural ramifications of social mobility, Goffman (1959) approaches the problem from an interactionist point of view, utilizing the metaphor of the theatrical performance as an explicatory device.

> One of the richest sources of data on the presentation of idealized performances is the literature on social mobility. In most societies there seems to be a major or general system of stratification, and in most stratified societies there is an idealization of the higher strata and some aspiration on the part of those in low places to move to higher ones. . . . Commonly we find that upward mobility involves the presentation of proper performances and that efforts to move upward and efforts to keep from moving downward are expressed in terms of sacrifices made for the maintenance of front. Once the proper sign-equipment has been obtained and familiarity gained in the management of it, then this equipment can be used to embellish and illumine one's daily performances with a favorable social style.[17]

The actual situation in societies characterized by rapid flux and expanding possibilities for personal mobility appears to be somewhat more complex than Goffman's statement suggests. The utility of the "proper sign-equipment" depends on its stability and continued applicability. Hammel (1964, p. 86) has pointed out that if the system of symbols of hierarchically organized statuses becomes less representative of those statuses, it signifies that these statuses are less distinguishable from one another in the messages exchanged between actors in the system. In such a case it may be presumed that effort will be expended to reestablish a consistency between the culture and the society. Hammal (1964, p. 87) comments that new behavior often must be acquired as a corrective device; that is, one must find new symbols appropriate to a given status to replace those which have been lost through intrasocietal diffusion. For example, it is my impression that in developing nations there is constant borrowing of new symbols from the West on the part of the upper strata. The educated classes have superior means to engage in this game since they often have knowledge of foreign languages, possess superior

---

[17]From E. Goffman, *The Presentation of Self in Everyday Life,* page 36. Doubleday & Company, New York 1959. © 1959 by Erving Goffman.

economic capabilities, and are able either to travel abroad or to maintain lines of communication with the outside world. As these new materials are diffused down the social scale, there is an almost frantic effort to replace them with new symbols.

Thus, individuals not only strive to take on cultural materials that are consistent with the statuses above them, and to slough off behavioral patterns associated with positions in the hierarchy which they perceive as less prestigious, but also attempt to maintain any advantage gained. However, perception of ascending-class behavior may often be incomplete, superficial, and inaccurate, and newly acquired symbols may frequently appear transparent or ludicrous to those with a greater range of competency within the total information system.

With these points in mind, the problems of geographic and social mobility will be examined in the context of the perceptions and expressed motivations of those who have personally, or whose parents have, migrated from villages and provincial towns to Yugoslavia's largest urban center, Belgrade. Questions will be examined regarding the behavior of those who have been called upon to operate in terms of both a traditional and a contemporary informational system. What are the ranges of competency exhibited within both spheres? Are these perceived as separate cultural entities, or as a single integrated whole within which individuals simply exhibit varying degrees of proficiency? Will those who show a high level of skill in manipulating the symbols of modern urban culture also have an adequate grasp of the traditional code; that is, does control of one segment of the culture presuppose that of another? What difficulties are experienced in the perception and emulation of ascending-class behavior? This study centers not so much on the nature of the various levels of culture as on the process by which persons pass from one stratum to another, and learn to control their new environment, balancing the advantages of innovation against the security and moral validation of traditional beliefs and relationships.

Methodology and Focus

Problems of methodology encountered by the anthropologist working in a complex urban setting are numerous. A lone investigator in a large city, such as Belgrade, cannot hope to explore the totality of the community's cultural and behavioral patterns, nor can he be intimately familiar with the full range of statuses typical of the society. However, the traditional approach of anthropology can yield detailed accounts of the life of specific segments of the population, as well as a picture of the environment as perceived through the eyes of the native.

An expectation of anthropological field work is that the researcher will, in addition to interviewing and observing, also become an actor within the social milieu in which he finds himself. He will, to a greater or lesser degree, share the life of his subjects, internalizing something of their values and assumptions. Bohannan (1963) sees anthropology, above all else, as a comparative science, and the ethnologist as "a translator of strange ideas, customs, and things into familiar language [p. 10]." To record and interpret accurately an exotic social system, one must become, in a sense, bicultural. This is seldom achieved deliberately, but comes about as the product of necessary daily activities, and through encounters typical of the flow of ordinary life: shopping, reciprocity with neighbors, ritual activities, and so forth. In other words, to operate in a culture with efficiency is to learn its norms and expectations. Steinbeck (1962), for example, in his American odyssey *Travels with Charley*, cites the value of such commonplace interaction and the observation of seemingly trivial detail as guides to the interpretation of the greater whole:

> Once I traveled about in an old bakery wagon, double-doored rattler with a mattress on its floor. I stopped where people stopped or gathered, I listened and looked and felt, and in the process had a picture of my country the accuracy of which was impaired only by my own shortomings. So it was that I determined to look again, to try to rediscover this monster land. Otherwise, in writing, I could not tell the small diagnostic truths which are the foundations of the larger truth [p. 5].[18]

The problem orientation of this study was formulated in a general way in the United States as the result of library research,

---

[18]From *Travels with Charley: In Search of America* by John Steinbeck copyright © 1961, 1962 by The Curtis Publishing Co., Inc., © 1962 by John Steinbeck. Reprinted by permission of the Viking Press, Inc.

and from the impressions of two previous sojourns in Yugoslavia. The exact focus and methodology, however, were the product of experiences and observations during the first few months of residence in Belgrade. Initially the tasks of finding housing, settling a family into a daily routine, and arranging for the admission of two children into local schools, together with the establishment of rapport with officials and Yugoslav social scientists, occupied the greater part of my attention. Through such purposeful activities and the interpersonal relationships engendered by them, I was able both to sample the general tone of life in the city and to expand the network of friends and acquaintances that had been originally established during visits to Belgrade in 1961 and 1966.

It was thus with a specifically interactionist orientation[19] that the problem of rural–urban migration and the question of culture change within the city itself was approached. This viewpoint persisted during the year of the study and provided the background for more formal methods of research. Belgrade furnished ample opportunities for observations and participation, probably to a significantly greater degree than a similar community in the United States since, due to a housing crisis and the nature of Serbian culture, there is a much broader range of life outside the home than in our own country. The American and northern European prohibitions against interaction with strangers, and meddling in the affairs of others in public places, do not exist, on the whole, in Yugoslavia. This increases the chances for both the scrutiny of, and the partaking in, casual encounters.

Much of the data for this study were derived from informal contacts which were often spontaneous and superficial in nature. These, for the most part, were not explicitly related to the conduct of the research, and the degree to which these encounters could be exploited was limited both by good manners and by the nature of boundary-setting and distance-maintaining mechanisms in the

[19]Interactionism has been frequently described as "an orientation not a theory." Goffman (1959), for instance, employs the idea of a theatrical performance as a framework for viewing human interaction, considering the manner in which individuals present themselves and attempt to control the impressions they give to others. For further elaboration see Blumer (1962), Cicourel (1964), and Coser and Rosenberg (1964, pp. 55–86), among others.

culture.[20] To have revealed my true purpose in the position of an "unknown quantity" would have, in many cases, aroused suspicion and precluded further communication. For example, a great deal of relevant material was gleaned from conversations with tradesmen, clerks, fellow passengers on public transportation, neighbors, and schoolmates of my children. Such "interviews" were essentially dominated by the respondents, with only subtle attempts on my part to introduce specific subject matter. However, I found that, allowed a position of dominance, even a virtual stranger was willing to reveal a great range and depth of personal information. The principal drawback to such an approach is the lack of comparability of much of the data so obtained.

A general format for a more consistent and formal approach to interviews was gradually evolved during the first three or four months of the study, and was developed in response to a growing awareness of the major areas of concern and focus within the culture. However, a problem was encountered in the sampling process since, outside of the framework of official projects associated with and carrying the prestige of formal Yugoslav institutions, random selection techniques are almost impossible. The principal difficulty stems from the attitudes of a public which is, for the most part, unfamiliar with such procedures. This same problem also constitutes an obstacle for native investigators, and in response to my complaints, a Yugoslav public health worker made the following observation.

> *Our people are in some ways very suspicious, especially those from the village who now reside in the city. You would have better luck on their own ground. I have many of the same difficulties in treating patients.*

Similarly, a Yugoslav sociologist told me that he had experienced

---

[20] For example, see Hammel (1967), who describes the traditional Serbian ritual of hospitality in which the guest is offered food and drink as soon as he is received in a household: sweet preserves of honey, a glass of cold water, brandy, and Turkish coffee. The author states, however:

> The warmth of the reception leads the ethnographer to assume that he has established rapport, but what he has established (or has been placed into) is a role—that of guest. The ritualized hospitality is, like much hospitality anywhere, a distance-maintaining and boundary-setting mechanism [p. 55].

resistance to interviewing even within the context of an official inquiry.

In selecting subjects for formal interviews, I initially turned to my personal network of friends and neighbors, who became the first families to be studied in depth. They, in turn, placed me in contact with other households and individuals. For example, an informant who coached an amateur basketball team was able to help me establish rapport with the families of several members of the club as well as with the janitor of the elementary school where the players trained. A large Belgrade construction company provided me with a list of workers who had been informed that they would be interviewed by an "American ethnologist."

There was a conscious effort to control the sample in such a way that it would represent a wide range of experience in the city. Thus, both natives of Belgrade and immigrants who had resided there for varying lengths of time were included. The time variable therefore exhibited two dimensions: one of individual and the other of generational depth of urban exposure. The informants also contrasted sharply in terms of their educational and occupational backgrounds; in spite of this, however, there was no family which did not have at least some distant tie to the countryside. At the same time, the sample was limited with a few exceptions to Serbians,[21] who represent the predominant population element in Belgrade. This also served the purpose of precluding the introduction into the study of variables of nationality and religion. (For a description of the characteristics of the sample refer to Appendix I.)

When possible, the formal interview, which required a minimum of two evenings per family to administer, was carried out with each member of a household. Though the interview format served as a general guideline, it was not possible to adhere to it strictly. My presence in the home of the informant placed me in the role of a guest, a subordinate position to that of the host, who maintained the prerogative of dominating the interac-

[21]For the purpose of this study, *Serbian* or *Serb* designates a Serbo-Croatian speaker of the Eastern Orthodox faith, or whose immediate ancestors were of that confession. Many Serbians reside outside the boundaries of the Serbian Republic in the other constituent Yugoslav republics, and are especially numerous in Montenegro, Croatia, and Bosnia–Herzegovina. In Serbo-Croatian *srbijanac* signifies a Serbian resident of Serbia proper, while *srbin* is a general term not specific to a particular geographic area.

tion. Unproductive lines of questioning were often abandoned in favor of more rewarding subject matter of greater interest to the interviewee.[22] Serbians do not, on the whole, respond well to a formal interviewing situation, and regard the activity as an opportunity for socializing rather than as a productive effort. When notes were taken in the presence of an informant, a common reaction was one of concern for "giving the right answer." For example, I was often questioned regarding what others had said, or as to "what was the correct reply?" Allowing the conversation to develop in a natural way, and at the pleasure of the respondents, proved to be the most workable technique.[23] Another difficulty revolved around the fact that it was rarely possible to interview individual household members in isolation.[24] Responses, therefore, represented in many cases a consensus of family opinion. This often precluded lines of questioning which, for example, centered on sex-role behavior or sexuality. It was, however, sometimes possible on subsequent occasions to arrange meetings alone with individual family members.

[22]For example, a simple test was devised, consisting of three pictures taken from popular magazines. These illustrations were conceived by the investigator as representing elements of traditional and modern culture. The informants were requested to make up a short story about each photograph indicating the statuses and emotional states of the individuals depicted. They were advised that the narration should have time depth, that is, it should show a progression from the past to the future. Although the informants were urged to give free reign to their imaginations, they generally refused to engage in speculations; rather, they meticulously enumerated exactly what they saw in each picture. Most reacted with embarrassment or nervous agitation to participation in the experiment. No matter how the test was described, there was a refusal to regard the illustrations as a kind of neutral ground for creativity and imaginative imagery. Similarly, Foster (1967b, p. 143) describes a case from Mexico where those to whom he had administered a Rorschach test were preoccupied with the answers those who preceded them had given.

[23]Berreman (1962, p. 21) recounts a similar problem in India where he often felt the need to conceal the extent of his note taking. Generally, the manner in which he was able to gather data was dictated by the cultural peculiarities of the Himalayan village in which he carried out his research. For example, he discarded plans to use scheduled interviews and questionnaires because he thought they would do more harm than good in terms of his rapport with the villagers.

[24]For example, I had invited an informant to come to my apartment so that he could be interviewed privately outside the context of his family, since I felt he would speak more freely away from the scrutiny of his parents. Though he had visited alone on many previous occasions, he pleasantly but stubbornly insisted that the interview take place in his own home. In several other cases informants were told that the interview would be more meaningful if conducted in private, but somehow other members of the family always managed to be present.

As time and circumstances permitted I attempted to maintain continued communication with the subjects of the in-depth studies so as to obtain further behavioral data and insight into the life styles of the participating families. Subsequent interviews permitted the elaboration of life histories and the taking of genealogies indicating the breadth of kinship relationships and knowledge. The frequency of contact with individual households varied from three occasions to over 300 in the case of a close neighbor.

Twenty-seven households consisting of 83 individuals provided the basis for the in-depth studies, while 74 persons participated in informal interviews. The question may well be raised whether a sample of 157 cases is an adequate one from which to draw general conclusions regarding a population of close to 1,000,000. In this respect, it should be pointed out that contemporary Serbian culture is still relatively homogeneous, and that even the urban elite have very recent roots in the peasantry. This is underscored by the fact that although the sample covered a wide range of Belgrade society, from peasant to professional, there was a surprising similarity between the responses of all interviewees. Moreover, it is the intent of this work to depict urbanization, rural–urban migration, and social mobility in terms of its qualitative aspects, as a human experience viewed through the eyes of some of the participating actors.[25]

---

[25]Weber, for example, believed that one of the possible approaches to the study of a society is through the individual, who as a member of a status group is the product of a social organization. Thus, the actions and ideas of individuals may be regarded as attributes of that social organization. He viewed society as an equilibrium between opposing forces and rejected any attempt to interpret social structures as wholes, at least in the context of sociological investigation. Sociology was for him a study of the understandable behavior of individuals in society. What the members of a society take for granted, even in their most ordinary behavior, in reality involves primary beliefs and assumptions without which they cannot function (see Bendix, 1962, pp. 260–267).

CHAPTER III

THE SETTING: HISTORICAL AND CONTEMPORARY PERSPECTIVES

Introduction

The relationship between the development of industry and technology and the growth of urban centers becomes apparent when we consider that the percentage of the world's population residing in cities of over 20,000 people increased from 2.4% in 1800 to 27.12% in 1960.[1] This trend has been especially pronounced in the so-called newly developing nations,[2] and the mas-

---

[1]See Hoyt (1962, p. 31) and United Nations Secretariat, Bureau of Social Affairs, in cooperation with International Labor Office, Food and Agricultural Organization, UNESCO, and World Health Organization (1957, p. 113).

[2]For example, the population in Asia living in cities of over 100,000 increased 444% between 1900 and 1950, while in Africa there was an increase in the same period of 629% (United Nations Secretariat, Bureau of Social Affairs, in cooperation with International Labor Office, Food and Agricultural Organization, UNESCO, and World Health Organization, 1957, p. 114).

sive population shifts that have occurred in Yugoslavia during the last 25 years reflect a worldwide phenomenon.

Yugoslavia emerged from the Second World War as one of the most agrarian and least urbanized countries in Europe (see Tables 1 and 2), and in 1960 still ranked with Albania, Malta, and Portugal as the only European nations with under 20% of their populations living in cities of over 20,000 people.[3] The South Slavs had entered the postwar period as a predominantly peasant and nonindustrial people[4] bearing the economic legacy of centuries of virtual colonial domination by the Ottomans and Austro-Hungarians. Neither the Turks nor the Hapsburgs had encouraged the development of native industry; the Turks lacked a predilection for commerce and trade, while the Hapsburgs supported the expansion of established industrial centers in Central Europe, drawing on their Balkan holdings for raw materials. Thus, Balkan industry was destined to remain, for the most part, stagnant at the folk craft and small-scale production level.[5] Though there were some ineffectual attempts at industrialization from about the mid-nineteenth century on,[6] these small gains were essentially wiped out by the economic crisis of the early thirties, and the destruction wrought during the Second World War.

[3]See United Nations Economic and Social Council (1965) for a worldwide comparison of levels of urbanization.

[4]Trouton (1952) describes the development of Yugoslavia from the turn of the century to the beginning of the Second World War in terms of its evolution from a "pure peasant to a mixed peasant society." During this period the South Slavs remained predominantly agrarian at the "market-town phase," but also began to exhibit some elements and institutions typical of the modern industrial state. Note that I have employed the term *intermediate society* in this work to designate a level beyond the incipient stage of industrialization described by Trouton. Intermediate society is applicable to Yugoslavia at its present state of development, where modern industrial production represents a significant proportion of the national product but a high percentage of the population (perhaps half) still pursues occupations related to agriculture.

[5]Economic life in Yugoslavia prior to the Second World War seems to have conformed quite closely to that of the preindustrial city as described by Sjoberg (1960, pp. 186–204). Commerce and labor enjoyed a low status; economic relations were personalistic and frequently a function of kinship; there was little job mobility; capital formulation was difficult; mass production and mass markets were lacking; there was little idea of supply and demand; universal standards of measurement and excellence were rare; and the work ethic was undeveloped.

[6]Trouton (1952, p. 54) comments that even Belgrade at the turn of the century "had only a handful of small-scale factories" and that outside Belgrade in Serbia there was only a government arms works at Kragujevac.

TABLE 1

Urbanization in Yugoslavia during the Postwar Period[a]

	1948	1953	1961
Population of Yugoslavia	15,842,107	16,991,449	18,549,264
Population in cities of over 20,000	2,272,647	2,661,122	3,478,743
Percentage of population in cities of over 20,000	12.5	15.7	18.8
Numbers of cities with populations over 100,000	2	5	7

[a]From *Socijalistička Federativna Republika Jugoslavija* (1965a, pp. xxii–xxiv).

TABLE 2

The Relative Importance of Agriculture and Industry in Terms of Employment in Yugoslavia and Its Constituent Republics in 1961[a]

Area	Percentage of population employed in	
	Agriculture	Industry
Yugoslavia	56.2	11.9
Serbia	62.5	9.8
Slovenia	36.6	22.7
Croatia	50.2	14.0
Bosnia and Herzegovina	58.1	9.8
Macedonia	58.2	8.7
Montenegro	53.6	8.8
Belgrade[b]	16.9	19.8

[a]From *Socijalistička Federativna Republika Jugoslavija* (1965b, pp. xxxi–xli).
[b]The *srez* (approximately equivalent to the American county) rather than the city proper is meant.

Following the war, the new Communist leadership embarked on an ambitious program of industrialization and modernization that made it possible for Yugoslavia to experience a rapid economic and social transition. Yugoslavia has, in fact, often been regarded as a model for other developing nations, and during the years 1957 to 1960 enjoyed one of the highest rates of economic growth in the world.[7] Development has been characterized by the expan-

[7]Fisher (1966, p. 2) cites the figure 13% as the rate of economic growth for the period of the Third Five-Year Plan, 1957–1960, as compared with a prewar figure of 1.9%. Hammel (1969b, p. 12), on the other hand, cautions that it is very difficult to

The constituent Yugoslav political divisions.

sion of basic industries and construction, accompanied by a shift away from dependence on peasant agriculture, which by 1964 accounted for only 20% of the national income.[8] Economic change also brought about mass migration from the countryside into the towns and cities, resulting in a rapid increase in the magnitude of urban centers. For example, Hoffman and Neal (1962, p. 485) estimate the level of migration to cities as 380,000 per year just after the close of the Second World War, and approximately 170,000 per year in the period from 1953 to 1957.

Perhaps nowhere else in the country have these momentous changes been so evident as in the nation's capital, and the choice of Belgrade as the site for a study regarding the cultural effects of modernization and industrialization reflects this realization as well as a number of other considerations. In many ways, the city typifies the transformations that have swept the South Slav lands during the nineteenth and twentieth centuries. At the time of

[8]Hammel (1969b, p. 10) cites these statistics regarding the percentage of the national income derived from agriculture: 1923, 52%; 1939, 44%; 1959, 29%; 1964, 20%.

assess accurate changes in the rate of growth of the Yugoslav economic system due to the paucity and frequent noncomparability of early statistics. For a detailed treatment of the history and development of the Yugoslav economy refer to Hoffman and Neal (1962), Kukoleča (1956), and Tomasevich (1955).

the first Serbian uprising against the Ottomans in 1804, Belgrade was little more than a dusty oriental market town with a Turkish garrison dominating the heights at the confluence of the Sava and Danube Rivers. During the nineteenth century, the Turks were gradually and completely expelled from Serbia proper, and Belgrade enjoyed moderate growth as both the intellectual and administrative center of the new Serbian state. A second period of expansion was to follow the First World War with the creation of the Kingdom of the Serbs, Croats, and Slovenes (later changed to Yugoslavia) with Belgrade as its capital. However, the city remained an essentially preindustrial community, a provincial center in a predominantly agrarian, peasant nation. The Second World War saw the loss of many of the small advances realized during the interwar era. The city was severely damaged, and its communications, industry, and sanitary facilities were almost completely destroyed. The outcome of the war totally altered the political structure of the nation, and brought about profound changes in the economic characteristics of Yugoslavia. This metamorphosis is evident in the recent history of Belgrade, which has been marked by intensive development, and a rapid increase in its physical and demographic dimensions. The city has grown far beyond its previous boundaries along the banks of the two great rivers, gradually encompassing nearby villages and farmlands. New settlements of high-rise apartments and numerous public buildings have displaced adobe-walled remnants of the Ottoman and Royal periods. Former swamps and expanses of shifting sands have become the sites of satellite communities. The influx of rural migrants has caused the population to more than double during the period from 1944 to 1962, and by 1969 the metropolitan area was approaching the level of 1,000,000 inhabitants (see Table 3).

Belgrade is both Yugoslavia's capital and its largest city. It is a hub of political and economic power, as well as a major center for innovation and the diffusion of new ideas. However, its role must be viewed in terms of the fact that it is difficult to regard Yugoslavia as a completely formed and integrated nation-state. Rather, it is best understood as several nations in the process of becoming a single cultural and political unit. Yugoslavia's historical development did not result in the appearance of a single

TABLE 3

Population Growth of Belgrade from 1910 to 1965[a]

Year	City only	Entire srez	Area not specified
1910	—	—	89,876
1921	—	—	111,740
1931	—	—	238,775
1937	—	—	385,000 (estimate)
1948	365,766	550,591	—
1951	437,641	643,190	—
1961	585,243	843,209	—
1965	697,000	—	—

[a]See *Direkcija Državne Statistike u Beogradu* (1924); *Kraljevina Jugoslavija Opšta Državna Statistika* (1939); *Socijalistička Federativna Republika Jugoslavija* (1965a); and *Socijalistička Federativna Republika Jugoslavija* (1969).

These statistics illustrate Belgrade's growth from a provincial town to an incipient metropolitan complex. Population statistics are not constantly comparable since there is often no indication whether figures are applicable to the city proper only, or also include its satellite communities and rural districts. For example, the figures for 1931 and 1937 probably include the entire Prefecture of Belgrade, whereas for 1948, 1951, and 1961 separate data are available for the city proper (including Zemun and New Belgrade but not Bežanija) and the *srez* (county).

primate city, but rather in the growth of several regional centers, each associated with a specific national entity and having its own specific social, political, and cultural characteristics. For instance, Zagreb, the nation's second city, is Western and Catholic, and Croats, regardless of their place of birth, look to it as a focus of ethnic identity.[9] Similarly, Ljubljana acts as a magnet for the Slovenes, Sarajevo for Slav Moslems, and Skopje for the people of the newly formed Macedonian Republic, whose population had long been torn between the territorial and political ambitions of Serbia and Bulgaria.

Belgrade is Eastern Orthodox, and traditionally Byzantine in custom and orientation. While it is the seat of national government, it is also the focal point of regional power and the locus of Serbian religious, cultural, and intellectual institutions. For both

[9]Fisher (1966, p. 54) attributes the reluctance of high-level professional and political leaders to leave Slovenia and Croatia for Belgrade to (among other factors) "great attachment to their native city, reinforced by a set of cultural attitudes that considers this attachment the normative pattern for a good Croatian or Slovenian."

intellectuals and peasants, Belgrade symbolizes the apex of Serbian accomplishment, and as Hammel (1969b) points out, "Belgrade is the final Yugoslav station on the Serbian road to success in migration [p. 25]."[10] Thus, Belgrade can be regarded as the focus of forces of both national unity and ethnic divisiveness. Significantly, the city also exhibits those opposing characteristics I have described as typical of intermediate societies. It is here that traditional values and modes of behavior contrast most sharply with elements of world culture, and come into conflict with the agents of change. While Belgrade is a funnel for the diffusion of traits from the outside world, it is simultaneously the subject of peasantization and further Serbianization through the influence of its own rural migrants.

Belgrade, due to its size and diversity, provides the optimal site in Yugoslavia for investigating the effects of social and spatial mobility, and the resultant dynamics of acculturation and culture change. It will logically evidence a broader spectrum of cultural patterns and a wider range of alternatives for individual behavior than smaller, provincial, industrial cities, which are more closely tied to the local hinterland and lack direct lines of communication to the national and supranational levels.

The South Slavs: Historical Perspectives

The very late appearance of urban life among the Balkan Slavs outside of Dalmatia has its origins in the earliest historical development of southeast Europe. These very same factors can also account for the only recent emergence of Yugoslavia as a growing industrial power. Yet it is not an easy task to summarize the past of the South Slavs, whose history does not form a consistent

---

[10]For example, Belgrade attracts large numbers of Serbian migrants from areas outside the Serbian Republic. The number of Montenegrins in the city is the subject of much levity since they are reputed "to control the bureaucracy," and their regional stereotype centers on an aversion to work. (In the popular lore of Zagreb the Dalmatians hold a similar position.) Fisher (1966, p. 54) comments that over 50% of Montenegro's Communist Party members reside outside the Republic, mainly in Belgrade. He attributes this to close cultural ties to the Serbs and the differential in the standard of living. It should be noted that, though they have a somewhat different historical tradition, and their own autonomous republic, the Montenegrins are generally regarded as being Serbs. Similarly, Dalmatians are considered Croats.

whole, but rather, one best characterized in terms of the disparate parts of a mosaic reflecting the centuries-long cultural and political marginality of the Balkans. Each Yugoslav republic exhibits the cultural legacy of a unique set of events bound to relationships with greater powers, and it is a tribute to the symbolic strength of language[11] that such diverse peoples have managed to create the even tenuous unity that has succeeded in joining them into a single incipient supraethnic state. In no country of Europe is the juxtaposition of contrasting elements so evident as in Yugoslavia, and indeed, no other European state outside the Soviet Unon shows greater ethnic diversity. If one were to seek a single strand or theme by which to characterize the past of the Balkan Slavs it would perhaps be the movement of peoples. Just as the modern Yugoslav industrial city is the product of the former villagers who abandoned their rural homes for the promise of urban life, much of Yugoslavia's past has been tied to the migrations of her population.

The Slavs were relative latecomers to southeast Europe, and when they crossed the Danube sometime during the fifth century as a barbarian wave from the northeast, they encountered the outposts of fully ripe and sophisticated civilizations. The Balkans had long been a region of human settlement, and much of the Neolithic population of Europe was probably derived from the east through the Balkan Peninsula.

The late Neolithic period in Europe was one of ethnic complexity. It was during this time of transition and migration that we can assume the spread of Indo-European speech into the Balkans. The earliest occurrence of Greek in southeastern Europe probably dates from the beginning of the second millenium B.C. Illyrians carrying the so-called Hallstatt Iron-Age culture spread southward from a focus in southern Germany and Austria along the eastern shores of the Adriatic, and had already begun settlement in the Balkans by the beginning of the first millenium B.C. It is a commonly held belief that the modern Albanians are in

---

[11]There are four official, or recognized, literary South Slav idioms: Slovene, Serbo-Croatian (Serbian and Croatian differ principally in that the former is written in Cyrillic characters and the latter in Latin letters), Macedonian, and Bulgarian. In actuality, the Balkan Slavs speak a continuum of dialects, all of which are to a great degree mutually intelligible.

part descendants of these early Illyrian settlers, or that in any case they represent an early Indo-European intrusion into the Dinaric highlands. Lying to the east of the Illyrians were the Thracians, a numerous people also speaking an Indo-European dialect and residing in the Balkans from early Hellenic times. Shortly after 500 B.C. the Celts introduced a new Indo-European strain, but were soon absorbed by the peoples indigenous to the peninsula.[12]

Classical Greek civilization developed against a background of ethnic heterogeneity, and the Athenian Greek was the product of the mixing of diverse populations. By the middle of the first millenium B.C. Greek influence was widespread throughout the Balkans, and Greek colonies dotted the Adriatic coast; among the most important were those at the sites of the present-day Dalmatian cities of Korčula, Hvar, Vis, Trogir, and Split.

It was not until after the third century B.C. that the Romans began to make their influence felt east of the Adriatic. Their hold became complete during the first years of the Christian era, and Latin culture left a profound imprint on the Balkans. In 9 A.D., Tiberius annexed and incorporated the Dinaric lands into the Roman Empire under the title *Illyricum*, a name which was to become a rallying cry for nineteenth-century South Slav nationalism.[13]

Of profound significance for the understanding of contemporary ethnic and religious differences in the Balkans is the division of the Roman Empire by Diocletian in 285 A.D. into an eastern and a western half. Though the Empire was reunited by Constantine for a brief period, there existed from 395 A.D. a definitive and fundamental cleavage between the civilizations of the East and West. The line of ultimate separation ran on a north-to-south axis from approximately Lake Skadar (Shkodër) to a point near

---

[12]Regarding the prehistory of the Balkans, see Coon (1939): Neolithic invasions (pp. 80–81, 101, 132–133); the Illyrians (pp. 182–186); the Thracians (p. 609); the origins of the Greeks (pp. 142–146). Also, refer to Ehrich (1965).

[13]In 1809 Austria was compelled to cede to Napoleon a large strip of territory in the western Balkans which he designated a single geographical unit, assigning it the ancient name of *Illyria*. Croats and Slovenes were thus brought briefly under one rule, and inspiration was generated for the *Illyrian Movement*, whose aims, though nationalistic, were primarily directed toward the intellectual, linguistic, and cultural unification of the South Slavs.

the confluence of the Sava and Drina Rivers.[14] In classical times this line corresponded roughly to a linguistic frontier between the Latin-speaking and Greek-speaking worlds; later it formed the boundary between Catholic and Orthodox Christianity.[15]

Roman power in the Balkans began to decline after the fifth century. The Goths had already penetrated the Dacian (Romanian) colonies by 256 A.D. and the Romans began a hasty departure from their eastern holdings. A succession of migrating peoples from the East—Huns, Slavs, Bulgars, Avars, and others —devastated the northern Balkans.

The appearance of the Slavs radically altered the future development and history of the Balkans,[16] and today, Slavic-speaking peoples form the largest single group in southeast Europe, controlling a geographical area of 141,562 square miles with a population of 26,000,000 (United Nations Statistical Office, 1964). Slavic dialects stretch from the northern Adriatic east to the Black Sea and south to the Aegean.

The Slavs had entrenched themselves in the Balkans during that period of history associated with the fall of the Roman Empire and characterized by numerous and complex migrations of peoples. Though the distinctions were somewhat obscure, the early South Slavs generally fell into four major groups: in the northwest, the Slovenes; to the immediate south, along the Adriatic Coast and in the Dinaric Mountains, the Croats; in the area directly south and east of them, the Serbs; and in the east bordering the Black Sea, the Bulgars.

The Balkan Slavs were gradually Christianized during the period from the seventh to the ninth century. Under the influence

[14]Regarding the exact frontier, Grafenauer *et al.* (1953) state, "The boundary between the two parts ran from Budva to the upper Drina, thence along the Drina to its confluence with the Sava, and then back down the Sava and Danube [pp. 49–50]."

[15]Modern ethnic and religious differences among the Balkan Slavs still reflect this early division.

[16]The original habitat of the Slavs is generally believed to have been northeast of the Carpathians, and to have extended as far east as the basin of the Middle Dnieper. They may have reached as far west as the Elbe, and as far north as the lands occupied by the ancestors of the modern Lithuanians in the basins of the Nieman and Dvina. At the beginning of the Christian era the Slavs probably represented a group speaking a single Slavic language of the Indo-European family. Regarding the early Slavs and their expansion south and westward, see Derzhavin (1946, pp. 7–161), Dvornik (1956), and Tret'yakov (1953, pp. 7–136).

of Rome and the Franks, the Croats and Slovenes gave their allegiance to the Pope. In contrast, after some vacillation, the Serbs and Bulgars finally accepted Christianity from Constantinople, and were drawn into the cultural sphere of Byzantium and the East. This early polarization of the South Slavs, toward Central Europe and Italy on the one hand and toward Byzantium on the other, has persisted to the present and is reflected in the contemporary ethnic and cultural composition of Yugoslavia and Bulgaria. For instance, the modern Slovenes evidence a cultural orientation determined by centuries of domination by the Franks, the Holy Roman Empire, and the Hapsburgs. Though the Croats also belonged to this sphere of influence, their cultural heritage also manifests a long history of close association with the Magyars, and intimate contact through Dalmatia with Italy and the Mediterranean. The Croats enjoyed greater autonomy during the Middle Ages than did the Slovenes, and in 924 were able to form an independent state under King Tomislav. Croat autonomy endured for nearly 200 years until 1091, when the rule of Croatia passed to King Ladislas of Hungary. This began an association between the two nations which, aside from occasional interruptions, lasted for over 800 years. In Serbia, the Nemanja Dynasty succeeded in building a medieval state which culminated in the empire of Stefan Dušan Nemanja (1331–1355), stretching from the Drina River to the Aegean and capable of challenging the power of Byzantium. Though Serbian culture was inseparably tied to Orthodoxy and the East, this early period was characterized by a struggle for religious and political autonomy from the Byzantines.

The appearance of the Turks in Asia Minor during the eleventh century sealed the fate of southeastern Europe. By the middle of the fourteenth century the Turks had subdued most of the Byzantine holdings in Asia, and by 1354 had established a beachhead in Gallipoli on the European side of the Dardanelles. The Ottomans soon poured into the Balkans, defeating a Serbo-Bulgarian coalition at the Battle of Maritza in 1371, and a few years later (in 1389), the Serbs on the Plain of Kosovo. Turkish domination in most of the Balkans was to endure until the nineteenth century, and in parts of Serbia, Macedonia, Albania, and Thrace until the First Balkan War of 1912.

The invading Turks brought about important movements of populations, pushing the South Slavs in a generally northward and westward direction away from the centers of Moslem power. The Vojvodina, an integral part of the Magyar lands lying north of the Sava and east of the Danube on the Hungarian Plain, was a focus for Serbian migration following the Battle of Kosovo, and by the sixteenth century Serbs formed nearly half of the population of this region. They were to provide the nucleus for a Serbian intelligentsia, with Vojvodina becoming the center of a national and literary revival during the late eighteenth and the early nineteenth centuries.[17] Many Serbs also fled westward into Bosnia, which did not fall to the Turks until after 1460. Croatia, too, received large numbers of refugees, since Ottoman control did not extend that far north until the early sixteenth century. Even then, Turkish power was tenuous in the Croatian and Hungarian lands, and by 1699 the Ottomans had ceded practically all of Croatia and Slovenia to the Hapsburg emperor. Now under Christian rule, these provinces increasingly acted as magnets for further Slav migration from the south. To the west the rugged Dinaric Mountains of Dalmatia, Lika, Herzegovina, and Montenegro provided another sanctuary for those who fled before the Moslem invader. Though the Montenegrins were frequently attacked by the Turks, they managed to retain a position of relative autonomy during the long Ottoman occupation of the Balkans. With the shift of the Serbian population northward into Croatia and Hungary and westward into the Dinaric highlands, the Bulgarians moved from the east into Macedonia, partially filling the vacuum left by the retreating Serbs. The Albanians, the majority of whom had been converted to Islam during the second half of the fifteenth century, also exerted pressure against the Serbs.

[17]The influence of the French Revolution and the German Romantic Movement reached the South Slavs principally within the framework of the Austro-Hungarian monarchy. Literary and linguistic revivals during the early nineteenth century were precursors of Yugoslav political independence. Important figures during this period were the Croat Ljudevit Gaj, associated with the Illyrian Movement (Ježić, 1944, pp. 198–288), and the Serbs Dositej Obradović and Vuk Stefanović Karadžić. The complete works of Obradović are contained in four volumes and include the author's autobiography (1961), which has been translated into English by Noyes (1953). Regarding Karadžić, who is considered the father of the modern Serbo-Croatian language and the founder of Serbian ethnography, see Kecmanović (1951). For a general review of South Slav language and literature, see Noyes (1949a,b).

Some Orthodox chose to become Moslem and Albanian, while others abandoned their homes and land to move northward. The principal thrust of Albanian expansion was into the regions of western Macedonia and Serbia (Kosovo), and southern and eastern Montenegro. Today Albanians comprise the majority of the population of Kosovo, and a significant minority in Macedonia and Montenegro.

The process of Islamization, which gradually spread over much of the Balkans under Ottoman domination, introduced a third major religious dimension to the ethnic fabric of southeast Europe. There was no need to impose the faith by force, since conversion often guaranteed a privileged social and economic position in the new society. In Bosnia, among the first to accept Islam were the adherents of the Bogomil heresy,[18] who were experiencing persecution from both Rome and Byzantium, and whose religious practices and tenets were in some ways similar to those of the Moslems. Many of the Bosnian nobility also accepted the belief of the conquerors to ensure their continued prestigious and dominant status. Bosnia remains the center of the Yugoslav Islamic community, though Slav Moslems are also found in considerable numbers in Montenegro, the Sandžak, Macedonia, and Bulgaria. (Regarding the distribution of confessions in Yugoslavia, see Tables 4A,B.)

A second significant feature of the Turkish occupation was its influence on the growth and development of urban life in central, southern, and eastern Yugoslavia. With the disappearance of the native Christian aristocracy the Slavs withdrew from the towns, and city life and culture took on an oriental aspect. Towns, under the Ottomans, acted as loci of military power, and often contained large garrisons. Political and social life was dominated by Turkish officers and administrative officials, while economics and trade were in the hands of a merchant class of non-Slavic

---

[18]The Patareni or Bogomils appeared in Bosnia during the twelfth and thirteenth centuries and are said to have taken their name from a Bulgarian priest of the tenth century, Bogomil (Beloved of God). Their creed held that the material world was the creation of Satan and that to escape his domination man must avoid all possible material contact and lead a life of asceticism. The Patareni rejected the Holy Cross, the Old Testament, and the sacraments, as well as the organization of the Christian Church. See Grafenauer *et al.* (1953, pp. 563–577). Regarding Yugoslav Moslems, see Vucinich (1949a).

TABLE 4A

*Distribution of Religious Confessions
in Yugoslavia in 1948[a]*

Religious group	Percentage
Eastern Orthodox	49.53
Roman Catholic	36.7
Moslem	12.62
Other Christian churches	1.14
Jews	0.04
Others	0.07

[a] From Darby, Stetson-Watson, Laffon, and Clissold (1966, pp. 241–242); Myers (1954, p. 51) indicates a slightly different distribution for 1948: Eastern Orthodox, 50.1%; Roman Catholic, 36.3%; Moslem, 12.1%; Protestant, 1.1%; others, 0.4%.

TABLE 4B

*Estimated Distribution of Religious
Confessions in Yugoslavia in 1953[a]*

Religious group	Percentage
Eastern Orthodox	51.34
Roman Catholic	35.06
Moslem	12.02
Other	1.58

[a] From Federativna Narodna Republika Jugoslavija (1960, pp. 416–417); the 1953 census does not give figures regarding religious affiliation, and the author has projected these percentages from the populations of the constituent ethnic groups of Yugoslavia.

origins.[19] Serbs who remained in urban centers, or who migrated to them, soon acquired values and mannerisms which sharply differentiated them from ther rural compatriots.[20]

---

[19] The merchant class in Serbia was composed principally of *cincari* (Tsintsars, a people by origin from Thrace, probably of mixed ethnic background), Sephardic Jews, Armenians, Greeks, and even Arabs. Trouton (1952, pp. 52–53) claims that the *cincari* spoke a dialect

The Turkish era can be characterized as one of stagnation of South Slav intellectual and economic life, and indigenous culture survived only among the clergy of the Orthodox Church, and on the folk level among the peasantry. As Turkish power waned during the eighteenth and nineteenth centuries, however, there was a rebirth of national feeling, accompanied by a new movement of populations down from the desolate mountain ramparts of the west, and eastward into the fertile valleys and lowlands of Serbia. The Serbs followed in the wake of the Turkish retreat, occupying what had become virtually virgin lands. For example, the modern population of western and northern Serbia is derived almost totally from migrations out of the Dinaric Mountains during this period.[21] Halpern (1958, pp. 9–11;) asserts that Šumadija, the heartland of Serbia stretching south from Belgrade to the Western Morava River, was largely deserted after the Turkish conquest during the fifteenth century, and that probably no more than 10% of the original population remained. By the nineteenth century, however, the area was permanently resettled by migrants from the Dinaric Mountains and the Vojvodina.

The First Balkan War of 1912 ended the last vestiges of Turkish power among the South Slavs, and the First World War put the finishing touches to the decline of another great empire with the expulsion of the Hapsburgs from Bosnia and Herzegovina, Croatia, and Slovenia. Unfortunately, the formation of Yugoslavia after the Great War, and the unification of the Slavs of the western Balkans into a single state did not signify the creation of a common national conscience. The interwar period was characterized by political instability, the collapse of parliamentary government, factionalism, ethnic rivalry, economic stagnation, and general backwardness in comparison to most of Europe.

[21]For instance, Barjaktarović and Pavković (1965) state that approximately 90% of the population of Jadar (a region in west Serbia centering around Loznica on the east bank of the Drina River) was derived since the eighteenth century from migrations out of the Dinaric highlands. For a general history of migrations in the Balkans from the Turkish period to the end of the Wars of Liberation, see Cvijić (1918, pp. 112–152; 1967).

of now extinct Thracian, which they abandoned for Slavic speech sometime after their arrival in Serbia at an unspecified date.

[20]Refer to Trouton (1952, pp. 50–54) regarding the oriental type South Slav urban center, the so-called *čaršija town*. For a description of the life of the Serbian bourgeoisie during the late Turkish period, see the novel of Stanković, *Nečista Krv* (Impure Blood) (1950).

The degree of internal dissension and the depth of ethnic and regional animosities became manifest during the period of the Second World War. The Germans and Italians, with their Hungarian and Bulgarian allies, attacked and occupied Yugoslavia in April of 1941 following a popularly based coup d'état against the government of Prince Paul, which had signed the Tripartite Pact with the Axis Powers. Yugoslavia was quickly defeated and partitioned, with the loss of large geographic areas adjacent to her victorious neighbors. Under German protection the Independent State of Croatia was established which included within its boundaries large Serbian and Moslem populations. Croatian extremists embarked on a program of persecution and terror against the Orthodox and Jewish communities residing within the territory controlled by the pro-Nazi regime. Though in a more limited scope, the Serbs responded in kind.[22] The war period saw the migration of many Serbs from the Independent State of Croatia and the Hungarian-controlled Vojvodina to the relative safety of German-occupied Serbia, which had been reduced to an area smaller than before the First Balkan War.

Against a background of factionalism and interethnic civil war, resistance to the German occupation solidified in the Communist-dominated Partisan Movement under the leadership of Tito. The efficient organization and military success of the Partisans, combined with their lack of identification with specific ethnic and religious groups, soon gave them a broader base of popular support than the proroyalist and highly nationalistic Serbian guerrillas of Draža Mihailović. By the time advancing Soviet armies had reached Belgrade, the Partisans had liberated most of Yugoslavia.[23] The end of the war found Tito's forces in control of the organs of government, and the new Yugoslav state was constructed on socialist and federal principles.[24]

---

[22]For a discussion of this period and the Independent State of Croatia, see Balen (1952).

[23]See Vucinich (1949b) regarding Yugoslavia during the second World War.

[24]Postwar Yugoslavia consists of six constituent republics: Serbia, Croatia, Bosnia and Herzegovina, Slovenia, Macedonia, and Montenegro (in order of size). These conform approximately to the distribution of South Slav ethnic and religious groups. In addition, there are two autonomous regions within the Republic of Serbia: Vojvodina (the site of large Hungarian, Slovak, and Romanian minorities) and Kosovo-Metohija (center of the Albanian minority in Yugoslavia). For a summary of the foundation of the Yugoslav socialist state, refer to Darby *et al.* (1966, pp. 236–264).

The immediate postwar period was characterized by a close association with the Soviet Union and the nations of the East European Communist Block. With Yugoslavia's expulsion from the Cominform in 1948 and Tito's break with Stalin, Yugoslavia embarked on a program of independent socialism, and a policy of neutrality and nonalignment in foreign affairs. The Yugoslav economy has been typified by the abandonment of forced collectivization of agriculture, decentralization, worker self-management, and limited private enterprise.

Following the war, the redistribution of agricultural land brought about renewed internal migration. The holdings of large landowners, collaborators, and expelled German settlers (*Volksdeutsch*) were parceled out to poor or landless peasants. For example, 385,000 hectares of land in the Vojvodina and the Sava Valley were given to peasant families from rocky, unproductive regions of Bosnia and the Dinaric Mountains (Darby *et al.*, 1966, pp. 240–241).

The new government's policy of industrialization also created another wave of internal migration. This movement was not in flight from enemies, nor in the quest of fertile land and more favorable conditions in which to pursue the traditional cultivation of the soil, but rather in search of the elusive vision of the twentieth century.[25]

Traditional Forms of South Slav Social Organization

The adaptation of the contemporary Serb to modern urban life in an increasingly industrial and money-oriented society cannot be adequately interpreted without some reference to the salient characteristics of traditional South Slav social organization. In this regard, Lewis (1952), in his study of Tepoztecan migrants in Mexico City, calls attention to the value of data regarding village culture and social structure as a "base line from which to analyze the nature and direction of change [p. 32]." Moreover, it is useful to examine constellations of community life in both their current rural variants and in terms of their historical antecedents. Dealing

---

[25]An accurate and well-organized resume of Yugoslav history is that of Darby *et al.* (1966). For more detailed accounts of South Slav history, see Grafenauer *et al.* (1953); Djurdjev, Grafenauer, and Tadić (1959); and Djurdjev (1961).

with the uses of history by anthropologists, Anderson (1971, pp. 1–8) notes that with anthropology's growing interest in the study of complex societies there has been an increasing similarity in the subject matter dealt with by both historians and anthropologists. Moreover, he suggests that the ethnographer in his analysis of literate societies may fruitfully turn to historical explanation as a valuable conceptual aid. Conversely, Anderson calls for "the application of specific anthropological concepts to limited historical problems." Thus, it is incumbent upon the anthropologist, where historical sources are available, to examine human behavior as the result of a continuing process, as well as in terms of the functioning of an ongoing sociocultural matrix.

When the Slavs first entered the Balkans as nomadic herders and casual agriculturalists (Grafenauer, Perović, & Šidak, 1953, pp. 71–72), they probably possessed a type of social organization very similar to that of other preliterate Indo-Europeans of the period. Their kinship structure appears to have been patrilineal with postmarital patrilocal residence and agnatically related families occupying contiguous territory or living in the same communities.[26] In the lowlands, along the periphery of the major area of Slav occupation, the social system probably underwent extensive changes due to close contact with neighboring peoples. On the other hand, in the core region of settlement the Slavs probably retained much of their original form of social organization.

Slavic tribes pushing westward during the period of their earliest settlement in the Balkans encountered aboriginal peoples, the most important of whom were the Illyrians and Thracians, who were either absorbed by or continued to live in proximity to the newcomers. The natives of the western Balkans (Illyria) were renowned in the Roman Empire as warriors, and they probably possessed social characteristics similar to those of the invading Slavs. Traditional South Slav society may well represent a synthesis

---

[26]Dvornik (1956, p. 57) describes the primitive Slavs as living in a communal landholding cooperative called the *zadruga*. At best, this appears to be speculative historical reconstruction, and it should be noted that the term *zadruga* was not originally a folk expression but was introduced into the folk system by Yugoslav ethnographers. Regarding early Slav social and political organization, refer to Dvornik (pp. 57–59). Grafenauer *et al.* (1953, pp. 72–73) also emphasize the communal character of primitive Slavic social organization within a framework of a patriarchal system based on kinship.

of several cultures, with changes in the Slavic social system reflecting ecological considerations and political exigencies.

Much of western Yugoslavia and Albania consists of *karst*, barren stretches of limestone mountains denuded, for the most part, of vegetation. In a few favored valleys (*doline*), and where the limestone crust has collapsed, forming depressions which have filled with soil (*polja*), there is sufficient fertile land to support small settlements. During the hot summer, water is scarce since the rains do not collect but rather penetrate the porous crust of the earth's surface and are lost. Such a natural environment cannot support a large population, and the history of these regions has revolved about the competition for scarce resources. Settlement is dispersed in isolated oases of fertility, with populations separated by a rugged, inhospitable, mountainous terrain almost totally lacking natural lines of communication.[27] It was in such an environment that classical Dinaric society took root and persisted for at least 1400 years.

Throughout centuries of Turkish domination, the Dinaric region of the Balkans remained generally outside the sphere of central political and military control, though there were sporadic attempts by the Ottomans, Venetians, and Austrians to bring the warlike mountaineers under their sovereignty. Even after the creation of the South Slav state following the First World War, control of these regions by the Yugoslav central government remained precarious. It was in these rugged highlands of the eastern Adriatic that a true tribal society persisted in Europe well into the twentieth century.

Dinaric society was strongly male oriented and reckoned descent patrilineally.[28] The smallest economically and politically significant social unit was the household (*kuća*), which comprised a minimal lineage known as the *familija* or *vamilija* (these terms can be roughly translated as "the family" or "the extended family"). The *kuća* generally consisted of a man and his wife; their unmarried sons and daughters; married sons with their wives and children; and sometimes married grandsons, or other close patrilat-

[27]Regarding the climate and geographical features of western Yugoslavia, see Taylor (1949). For a description of the physical characteristics of Montenegro and Albania, refer to Naval Intelligence Division (1920).

[28]The general outline of this discussion of traditional South Slav social structure follows closely that of Hammel (1968, pp. 13–37; 1969c, pp. 80–90).

eral male kin. Separate nuclear families maintained their own hearths within a common residence, and thus remained independent units of consumption. Physically, houses were often extended along a lineal axis to accommodate additional conjugal groups. Many such buildings can still be seen today in the Dinaric area, and the growth of the minimal lineage is clearly visible on the external facades, since each new addition deviates slightly in terms of materials, mode of construction, or coloring from the previous one.

The herding of sheep and goats, supplemented by the raising of a few cattle and the practice of limited agriculture where possible, formed the economic base of the society. Upon marriage, sons were usually given a share of their father's herd, which bestowed a degree of economic independence, though members of the *Kuća* continued to pasture their animals together. The cycle of fission and fusion of the household was rather short, and upon the death of the father, or when grandchildren had reached adulthood, it would split up, with some males remaining in the area and others migrating to establish new homesites at some distance. This process is quite explicable in terms of the limited resources available in a single region, population growth, and the pressure of migrants from the lowlands fleeing from Turkish domination.

Closely related households formed middle-range lineages called *porodice* (pl. of *porodica*, derived from the Serbo-Croatian *roditi*, to give birth). The *porodica* was generally based on ties between first and second patrilateral parallel cousins. In turn related *porodice* were bound together into maximal lineages called *bratstva* (pl. of *bratstvo*, brotherhood). These often exhibited as many as 10 or more generations of descent from an eponymic ancestor. The *bratstva* were loosely bound into tribes, *plemena* (pl. of *pleme*, tribe), each occupying contiguous territory, and utilizing common grazing and pasture lands. Though the *pleme* was usually a unit of territoriality rather than kinship, it sometimes consisted of several *bratstva* reputing distant agnatic ties. Unrelated *bratstva* were often bound to each other by marriage, ritual sponsorship at marriage and baptism (*kumstvo*), and blood brotherhood (*pobratimstvo*). Within a tribe, the influence of a *bratsvo* was related to its size in terms of adult male members, its economic position, and the nature of its alliances. Tribal unity was ephemeral, and the *plemena*, when not engaged in external warfare, were frequently torn by dissension and the blood feud (*krvna osveta*).

Membership in the *bratstvo* was symbolized by reputed descent from a common ancestor, patrilineal inheritance of a surname derived from the given name of the eponymic founder of the lineage (thus, Marković from Marko, "Mark"), exogamy, the observance of a common festival commemorating the conversion of the brotherhood to Christianity (*krsna slava* or *krsno ime*), and collective responsibility in ritual sponsorship and the feud. As a *bratstvo* grew in depth and breadth, segments of increasing independence and power might split off, forming a new brotherhood reckoning descent from a more recent genealogical point. Conversely, weak or small lineages might combine with stronger ones, abandoning their own name and *slava*, and taking those of a more powerful group.

In Dinaric society[29] prestige and authority were determined on the basis of age and sex, with the male principle dominant. In men, honor (*čast*) and heroism (*junaštvo*) were regarded as supreme virtues, while warfare and violence were accepted and socially sanctioned patterns of behavior. Sexual morality was strict, with faithfulness in marriage the norm (Erlich, 1940, 1966). Descent was not reckoned through women, and the uterine line was referred to as *tanka krv* (thin blood). Outside of linens, bedding, and a few personal effects, women brought no dowry into marriage, and received no inheritance from their fathers. Moreover, Serbian kinship terminology clearly differentiates most matrilateral from patrilateral kin, underscoring the stress on patrilineality.[30]

The decay of the Ottoman Empire and the decline of Turkish power in the Balkans saw the return of populations from the inhospitable western mountains down into the fertile and relatively uninhabited lowlands. The resettlement of these rich, productive

---

[29]Regarding Dinaric society and culture, see Coon (1950); Cvijić (1918, pp. 282–299); Djilas (1958); Durham (1904, 1909, 1928); Erlich (1966, pp. 379–396); Hasluck (1954); Simić (1967); and Tomasic (1948).

[30]For a description of Serbian kinship terminology, see Hammel (1957) and Halpern (1958, Fig. 24). Though both sources are incomplete, and Hammel's work represents a synthesis of the usages of several regions, a good general picture can be obtained from these works.

areas was accompanied by modifications in the traditional Dinaric tribal system in response to new conditions of life. An abundance of rich land and a plentiful supply of water made larger households possible, and families were able to remain more permanently in one location without fission and the dispersion of their members. The political function of the lineage and tribe declined, and was replaced by a village structure based on patrilocally extended households bound together by contractual ties. Villages were frequently composed of clusters of agnatically related households, since brothers often chose to settle near one another. The large numbers involved in migration, the shifting and mixing of populations combined with increasing control exercised by external political forces precluded the proliferation of the former societal type into a large-scale agnatic organization. However, many features of the previous society persisted. The stress on ties of kinship remained a focal value, as did a strong agnatic bias, and emphasis on corporate responsibility within the kin group.

The basic property-owning group was the patrilocally extended family, the *zadruga*.[31] It might consist of a father, his sons, and their wives and children, or it could be a fraternal joint-family of several brothers with their wives and children. Each *zadruga* had its roots in a nuclear family, and expanded by a simple extension of personnel and property until it became unwieldy. The size of the joint-family might grow to as many as 100 or so members, though this was unusual.

The *zadruga* held land, stock, water rights, tools, and other material goods in common. It was in every sense a family corporation united in common production and consumption. All adult males were voting members, with shares for inheritance reckoned by generation. Women inherited only if there were no sons and daughters otherwise married out. A brotherless daughter would frequently bring in a husband who became a fictive member of her patriline (*domazet*).

Members were normally coresident, and the house was divided into separate sleeping quarters for nuclear families. Young couples often occupied outbuildings or sleeping huts (*vajati, ajati*). At times members might leave as migrant workers, but in such

[31]For a discussion of the *zadruga* see, among others, Halpern (1958, pp. 134–150; Halpern and Anderson (1966); Mosley (1940, 1943, 1953); and Trouton (1952, pp. 27–33).

cases their wives and children remained behind, and membership in the corporation was not jeopardized.

Authority and prestige were determined, for the most part, by sex and age. The work and affairs of the *zadruga* were planned and coordinated by a single, capable, elder male (*starešina*), and a woman of advanced years, usually the *starešina's* wife, supervised the activities of the women. The division of labor was also generally determined by sex and age, though large *zadruge* (plural of *zadruga*) might also possess craft specialists.

The corporacy of the *zadruga* was clearly reflected in ritual life and in the common possession of nontangible property. The celebration of the *krsna slava* continued as in the Dinaric highlands. Though each household held a separate festival, the *slava* also symbolized recognition of membership in a maximal lineage composed of a number of family corporations (which, however, no longer held political significance). Thus, males celebrated the *krsna slava* of their fathers, and women often returned to their natal homes at the time of the commemoration of their patriline. Prohibitions against marriage with agnatically related kin persisted, as did the patrilineal inheritance of a lineage name. The blood feud, on the other hand, disappeared due to the decreased political importance of the lineage, the loss of tribal organization, and the extending influence of central government.

Ties of fictive kinship were not established between individuals, as in most of the Mediterranean and the West, but rather between *zadruge*.[32] The role of the individual was that of a representative of his corporate group, and patterns of participation in crisis rites were similar to those in production and consumption. Within the framework of sex and age there was a high level of substitutability of individuals within the *zadruga*. The holding of ritual sponsorship was regarded in the same way as the possession of property and followed the same patterns of inheritance as did the last name, the *slava*, and material wealth.

The *zadruga* is best viewed from the perspective of time depth, as a process, not a thing. It was a family institution with a rather long cycle of development when judged by western European standards. When the size of the *zadruga* became unwieldy, fission

---

[32]Regarding fictive kinship in the West, see Foster (1953b), Mintz and Wolf (1950), and Moss and Cappannari (1960).

would begin.[33] The immediate causes of dissolution lay within its very structure. For example, women often brought separate resources into marriage and disputes frequently centered around wives, who by birth were not bound together by membership in a single lineage as were the men. Other problems centered around differential inheritance related to the number of inheriting grandchildren, too much or too little land, and questions of authority and individualism. Fission was often a lengthy process, and was preceded by the gradual formation of separate loci of residence by nuclear families. Fathers frequently tried to keep the zadruga together until death and, anticipating fission, gave their sons residence plots upon marriage. A formal ceremony finalized the division of the zadruga, and if the father were still alive, he would often remain with one of his sons. Cooperation did not cease with fission, and brothers or cousins who continued to live in proximity would exchange goods and labor, and even share equipment and work animals.

The zadruga and Dinaric tribal society were the dominant forms of rural Serbian social organization until the period of the First World War. The increasing importance of a money economy and the growing influence of a central government, combined with improving means of communication, tended to erode traditional institutions. While the zadruga has not disappeared from the Yugoslav rural scene, there has been a decrease in its size, and today extended households of more than 20 members persist in only a few parts of the country. These occur principally in western Serbia among the Albanian minority, though they are not unknown in the region of Belgrade. Halpern (1958, p. 135) cites an example from the village of Orašac in Šumadija of a zadruga of two households consisting of 22 members.

Though households are smaller, the developmental cycle of the family shorter, and contemporary village life more individualistic than in the past, elements of corporacy and its associated values linger on. Although communal patterns of production and consumption no longer bind together large groups of agnatically related kin, and the blood feud has all but vanished from the Dinaric highlands, there remain strong feelings of collec-

[33]See Hammel (unpublished) regarding the cycle of lineage fusion and fission in southern and eastern Yugoslavia.

tive responsibility and representation, as well as a firm moral imperative regarding kinship relationships.[34] Though women have gained increasing independence, and by law inherit equally with male siblings, in practice they are, at least publicly, deferential and submissive, and seldom if ever accept land as dowry if there are inheriting brothers.

Industrialization and urbanization in Yugoslavia have made possible the reduction of excess rural population, and have created new lines of communication between city and village. While guidelines for behavior have been restructured and adapted to changing economic and social conditions, village life has remained, for the most part, within the familiar time-tested framework of traditional community organization. Moreover, these same principles will be shown to have influenced the course of urban life and culture in the new socialist state.

Belgrade: Past and Present

Just over 100 years ago Ali Rizah Paša, by order of the Sultan, handed over to Prince Mihailo Obrenović of Serbia the Kalemegdan Fortress, thus ending the last vestige of Turkish rule in Belgrade. Surprisingly, the modern city evidences few monuments suggesting this very recent oriental past. During the eighteenth century over 20 mosques with their slender minarets graced the skyline,[35] whereas today only one, the Bajrakli Džamija, remains, hidden on a quiet, tree-shaded back street of the old Dorćol District. The contemporary town is the product of an extraordinary metamorphosis accomplished in the span of a little over a century, and reflects the zeal of the builders of the Serbian state, who were determined to create a "European" capital for the young kingdom. Architecturally, modern Belgrade is an incongruous conglomerate of nineteenth-century European neoclassicism, Austrian Baroque, revivalistic pseudo-Byzantine, and twentieth-century glass and concrete superimposed on Islamic market town and Balkan village.

[34]Regarding adaptations in the Yugoslav kinship system related to contemporary social change, see Barić (1967a, b). Refer to Halpern (1958) for a general picture of contemporary Serbian village life.

[35]For a description of Islamic religious architecture in Belgrade, see Nikić (1958).

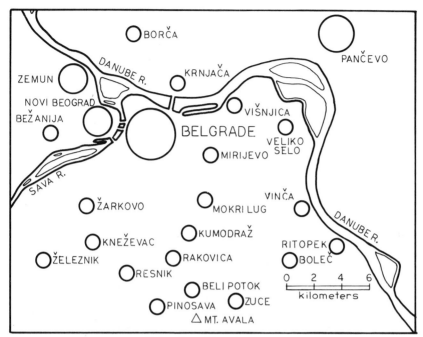

Belgrade and its surroundings.

The recent origins of much of the city belie the fact that this is among Europe's oldest locations of human settlement. Archaeological finds at such sites as Vinča, Kalemegdan, Banjica, Žarkovo, Rospi Ćuprija, and others establish Belgrade as a locus of community life during the Neolithic and in preclassical times.[36]

The Celts were the first known people to have constructed a permanent settlement at the confluence of the Sava and Danube Rivers sometime during the third and fourth millenia B.C. The city's first recorded name, Singidunum, by which the Romans called it, was probably of Celtic origin.

Belgrade's history has largely been determined by its strategic location, spread over numerous hills at the intersection of two great waterways. Today the capital's most noteworthy monument from the past is the Kalemegdan Fortress, perched on a limestone bluff overlooking the Sava and Danube. The city was destined to remain for most of its history a frontier outpost and military

---

[36]See Gavela (1958) regarding Neolithic sites in the environs of Belgrade.

bastion on the outer fringe of great civilizations. Belgrade was destroyed not once but many times, with each new conqueror plundering and burning what his predecessor had left.

The Romans held Singidunum for approximately four centuries during the early Christian era, but today this is evidenced by only a few sparse archaeological finds: sarcophagi, burial ornaments, graves, and a Roman bath on the site of the contemporary Students' Square (*Studentski Trg*). With the division of the Roman Empire, the town became a Byzantine frontier outpost looking across the Hungarian Plain from which were to arrive waves of barbarian invaders from the East. In the fifth and sixth centuries the Huns and Avars devastated the stronghold, and the migrating Slavs found the citadel in ruins. The Slavs, perhaps catching a glimpse of the white ramparts in the distance, called the city *Beograd* (white citadel). This name was first mentioned in a ninth-century Slavic manuscript, the biography of the monk, Kliment of Ohrid.[37]

Until the thirteenth century Belgrade remained outside the sphere of Slavic influence in the Balkans passing under the control of a succession of Hungarian, Bulgarian, and Byzantine administrators. During the fourteenth and fifteenth centuries the city was ruled alternately by the Hungarians and Serbs. After the Serbian defeat at Kosovo (1389), Belgrade became the capital of Despot Stevan Lazarević, who governed there until his death in 1427, when the Hungarians again asserted their dominance.

For Europe, alarmed at Moslem inroads toward the heart of the continent, Belgrade was one of the farthest outposts of Christianity and a bastion against the Turks. After a series of attacks and seiges, the city was lost to Suleiman the Magnificent in 1521, after which it remained under Ottoman control for three and a half centuries.

Belgrade became the largest and most important Turkish settlement in the Balkans and served as a base for expeditions to the north. The conquerors were aware of the city's strategic significance and called it *Darul al Džihad* (City of the Holy War).

---

[37]Kliment Ohridski, a disciple of St. Methodius, describes how he was driven out of Moravia by the German priesthood, and on his return trip to Bulgaria came upon "Belgrade, the most glorious city on the Danube. . ." (885 A.D.); see Paunović (1968, p. 82).

Belgrade was besieged and captured three times by the Austrians who, in one case managed to hold it for 22 years (1717–1739). With these exceptions, however, the Turks remained in undisputed dominance until the nineteenth century.

Under Karadjordje, the leader of the First Serbian Insurrection, Belgrade fell to the insurgents in 1806, and the city remained in Serbian hands until 1813, when the uprising was finally quelled by the Turks. The capital came permanently under the rule of the Serbs during the Second Insurrection which lasted from 1815 to 1817, though a Turkish garrison remained stationed in the Fortress for another 50 years.

By the beginning of the nineteenth century, reflecting the disintegration of the once powerful Ottoman Empire, Belgrade had declined from her former state of grandeur as a major Islamic city during the seventeenth century. The conquering Serbs found the city in ruins, with virtually no public services or sanitary facilities. Of the numerous mosques, only one was in use for religious services, and others had been converted into workshops, warehouses, or even stalls for animals. A few Turkish baths (*amami*) and inns (*hanovi*) continued to function. Commerical life consisted, for the most part, of the activities of small traditional craftsmen (*zanatlije*) and cafe keepers (*kafedžije*). The city presented the aspect of a typical Eastern town, with steep winding alleyways of Turkish cobblestone (*turska kaldrma*), occasional fountains (*česme*) from which the populace drew its water supply, and tile-roofed two-storied adobe-walled dwellings in Islamic style. European dress was conspicuously absent from the streets, and the Christian population affected Turkish styles or wore the costume of the local peasantry. The city was divided into three sections: The Fortress of Kalemegdan (*tvrdjava*); the town (*varoš*), which was further differentiated internally into ethnic quarters; and the satellite communities (*predgradja*) outside the earthen ramparts (*bademi*) which surrounded the *varoš*. The principal arteries into the city, which probably existed since Roman times, connected the town with the outside world through four major gateways (*kapije*) in the battlements. Life centered around a large central marketplace and bazaar (*čaršija*), called Zerek, located at the site of the present-day Students Square near the heart of the former *varoš*. The population was a mosaic of peoples, since Belgrade had long been

TABLE 5

*Religious Composition of the Population
of Belgrade in 1838[a]*

Religion	Numbers in population
Christians	8,483
Moslems (Turks)	2,700
Jews	1,500
Others	250

[a]From Andrić, Antić, Vaselinovič, and
Burić-Zamolo (1967, p. 69).

a magnet for migration not only from Serbia but from the whole
Balkan Peninsula and Anatolia as well. Numerous ethnic groups
shared the city: Serbs, Turks, Greeks, Iberian and other Jews,
Gypsies, Albanians, Bulgars, and Tsintsars.[38]

The nineteenth century saw the rapid expansion of Belgrade
as the political and cultural center of the new Serbian kingdom.
This period was one in which the city experienced what was at
least a superficial Europeanization of public and private life. At
the same time, the capital became an increasingly Serbian city
due to the absorption and emigration of minorities. There was
a steady decline in the Turkish and Moslem population, and by
1838 Christians already outnumbered the adherents of Islam by
more than three to one (see Table 5). This trend was to continue,
and before the turn of the century Belgrade had become, and
was to remain, overwhelmingly Eastern Orthodox in religion and
Serbo-Croatian in speech (see Tables 6 and 7). An exception to
this general trend toward ethnic and religious homogeneity has
been the growing migration of Albanian Moslems (*šiptari*) to the
capital from western Serbia (Kosovo) since the close of the Second
World War; at present they may number several tens of thousands.

As Belgrade grew in population, its boundaries expanded
beyond the limits of the old *varoš*, encompassing former satellite
communities and nearby peasant villages. The number of inhabitants increased markedly during the eighteenth century, and by

[38]Regarding Belgrade at the time of its liberation from the Turks, see Andrić *et
al.* (1967, pp. 32–38).

TABLE 6

Religious and Ethnic Composition
of the Population of Belgrade in 1924[a]

	Numbers in population
Religion	
Eastern Orthodox	95,205
Roman Catholics	9,203
Jews	4,800
Protestants	948
Greek Catholics	133
Moslems	1,316
Others	86
Nationality	
Serbo-Croatians	97,929
Slovenes	1,230
Other Slavs	3,103
Germans	3,677
Hungarians	1,346
Albanians	528
Others	3,827

[a]From Direkcija Državne Statistike u Beogradu
(1924, pp. 4–5).

TABLE 7

Ethnic Composition of Belgrade in 1953[a]

Nationality	Numbers in population
Total	470,172
Serbs	380,478
Croats	28,925
Slovenes	9,657
Macedonians	8,733
Montenegrins	11,365
Yugoslavs (unspecified)[b]	2,853
Albanians (*šiptari*)	3,687
Bulgarians	604
Vlachs	65
Turks	696
Other Slavs	6,328
Others	16,581

[a]From Federativna Narodna Republika Jugoslavija (1960,
p. 421).
[b]A category usually referring to Serbo-Croatian-
speaking Moslems.

1867 the figure had climbed to over 24,000, not quite double what it had been in 1846 (Andrić *et al.*, 1967, p. 69).

The Serbian insurrections, which had broken the back of Ottoman power and destroyed the Turkish feudal regime in the central Balkans, had also created the foundations for the expansion of an incipient capitalist system and the growth of a small native middle class and intelligentsia. Europeanization had begun to be felt by all segments of Belgrade society, and by the close of the century even the physiognomy of the city had been transformed on a Western model. Belgrade entered the twentieth century with water and sewage systems; straight, paved streets; streetcars; and an urban nucleus which physically resembled Vienna, Budapest, or Paris more closely than it did Istanbul.

The establishment of banks and the development of foreign trade contributed to the growth of a money economy and drew Serbia into the sphere of European financial interests, which nevertheless failed to contribute to the development of basic industry. Though there were some small first steps toward the creation of a native industrial base, it was the expansion of crafts and small business that laid the foundation for the Serbian bourgeoisie. For instance, the number of Belgrade guilds (*esnafi*) increased from about 30 in 1826 to 61 by 1847.[39]

The nineteenth century saw the proliferation of elementary and secondary schools, as well as the founding of institutions of higher learning. Drawing on both medieval Serbian and contemporary Western sources for style and inspiration, a native literary and artistic tradition developed along European lines. Belgrade rapidly became the center of Serbian intellectual and creative life,[40] as well as a symbol of Serbia's emergence from centuries of Islamic bondage into the currents of European life. However, the symbol and reality were not totally congruent, and Westernization was frequently superficial, a facade only partly obscuring what remained a fundamentally Eastern mentality.

The outbreak of the First World War, initiated by Austria's

[39]Andrić *et al.* (1967, pp. 61–70) discuss the economic role of Belgrade in the Serbian state during the nineteenth century, and the growth in the number of craft guilds (p. 61). Also, see the records of the Belgrade Court, 1819–1839 (Peruničić, 1964, pp. 269–354) regarding the number and variety of guilds in Belgrade in 1826.

[40]Regarding the development of the Serbian intelligentsia and the formation of a creative elite during the nineteenth and twentieth centuries, see Nemanjić (1964).

attack on Serbia, interrupted the city's development. Belgrade was besieged, and despite a heroic defense lasting over a year, Austrian and German troops entered the capital in September of 1915.

Following the defeat of the Central Powers, Belgrade began a new phase as the capital of the infant South Slav state. Though its growth continued during the interwar period, it was for the most part along lines laid down during the nineteenth century. The city remained a somewhat drab provincial replica of grander urban centers in the West. The veneer of urbanism and cosmopolitanism barely obscured the city's peasant and rural foundations.[41] Industry showed few advances, and Belgrade society had become top-heavy with petty bureaucrats and corrupt officialdom that stood in sharp contrast to an impoverished intelligentsia and proletariat.[42]

Once again external forces and events influenced the fate of the Serbs and their capital when, on Palm Sunday in April of 1941, without a declaration of war or any warning, German aircraft attacked Belgrade, killing thousands and leaving much of the city in ruins. Perhaps no other European nation suffered more severe damage or lost a greater percentage of her population in the Second World War than did Yugoslavia.

Belgrade was quickly occupied by the Nazis, and was only liberated during the closing moments of the war. Moreover, the city sustained further destruction during the course of the struggle from Allied air strikes and the heavy fighting that took place

---

[41]Rebecca West (1968), in comparing Belgrade with London, Paris, and New York, describes an incident in a pretentious Belgrade hotel on the eve of the Second World War:

> But in none of those great cities have I seen hotel doors slowly swing open to admit, unhurried and at ease, a peasant holding a black lamb in his arms. He took his place beside the news-stand where they sold *Pravda* and *Politika*, the *Continental Daily Mail, Paris Soir,* the *New York Herald Tribune.* He was a well-built young man with straight fair hair, high cheekbones, and a look of clear sight. His suit was in Western fashion, but he wore also a sheepskin jacket, a round black cap, and leather sandals with upturned toes; and to his ready-made shirt his mother had added some embroidery. [From *Black Lamb and Grey Falcon* by Rebecca West, page 483. Copyright 1940, 1941, © 1968 by Rebecca West. Reprinted by permission of The Viking Press, Inc.]

[42]During the interwar period political authority in the new Yugoslav state became increasingly concentrated in Belgrade, while Zagreb showed the greatest accumulation of wealth of any Yugoslav city, containing approximately 50% of all capital (Fisher, 1966, pp. 42, 51).

TABLE 8

Important Dates in the History of Belgrade

500 B.C.	Celtic settlements on site of present-day city
100 A.D.	Beginnings of Roman rule—city called Singidunum
450	Attila the Hun captures city
540	Byzantine Emperor Justinian rebuilds city
600	Avars capture and burn city
650	Permanent Slavic settlements in environs of city
885	First mention of present name of city, Alba Graeca (White Citadel—*Beograd*)
1070	Hungarians capture city from Byzantines
1284	First Serbian rule of city
1427	Hungarians capture city
1521	Turks, under Suleiman the Magnificent, capture city
1688	Austrians capture city
1739	Treaty of Belgrade—city returns to Turkish rule
1789	Austrians capture city
1791	Treaty of Sistova—Belgrade returns to Turkish rule
1806	Serbian insurgents under Karadjordje capture city
1813	Turks recapture city
1841	Belgrade becomes capital of Principality of Serbia
1867	Turks surrender their last stronghold in city, Kalemegdan Fortress
1914	Austrians capture city during First World War
1918	City becomes capital of the Kingdom of the Serbs, Croats, and Slovenes
1929	City becomes capital of Yugoslavia
1941	Germans capture city—end of the monarchy
1944	Liberation of city by Yugoslav Partisans and the Red Army
1945	Proclamation in Belgrade of the formation of the new Yugoslav socialist state

in and around the capital as Partisans and Russian troops drove out the Germans in October of 1944.

Following the close of hostilities, Belgrade rose from ruins to witness a new period of change and growth as the capital of the new Yugoslav socialist state. The face of the city was soon to be transformed by the construction of high-rise apartments, factories, and commercial and government buildings.

The speed of construction reflected an acute shortage of housing brought about by the war's devastation and the rapid influx of migrants attracted by burgeoning industry and increased economic opportunities. Style was frequently sacrificed to expediency, and on former marshes and empty fields dreary blocks of mass housing rose, multistoried and rectangular, lacking both grace and color. As in the past, the city reached out to encompass nearby villages and agricultural lands. Across the Sava, along the west bank of the Danube, in an area of shifting dunes and swamps arose New Belgrade (*Novi Beograd*), a twentieth-century suburb of uniformly stark concrete, metal, and glass. This tiringly symmetrical appendage of the capital was a response to the exigencies of a ballooning population and the need for obvious symbols of progress by a new government bent on bringing its people into the contemporary world.[43]

Belgradians often compare their city to Rome, claiming that in like manner it was founded on seven hills. In popular speech citizens orient themselves in terms of these landmarks: Kalemegdan, Terazija, Vračar, Zvezdara, Voždovac, Topčidersko Brdo, and Dedinje. Complementing the heights, seven valleys are said to lie at their feet: Dorćol, Savski Venac, Palilula, Bulbulder, Karaburma, Dušanovac, and Senjak. This bit of folklore conveniently omits other popularly designated districts that would conflict with the intent of the comparison (see Table 9 for the popular and administrative divisions of Belgrade).

Contemporary Belgrade reflects the transitional nature of the Yugoslav nation; it is not a single cultural and social entity but rather several, superimposed and coexisting in time and space. Despite the increasingly numerous modern monuments of the industrial age, the city's core, stretching southward from the ramparts of Kalemegdan Fortress, remains stolidly nineteenth century. The wide tree-lined boulevard of the Terazija bustles with activity, and is the noisy focus of the capital's commercial life. Within an area of perhaps less than 20 square blocks lies the hub of the present-day city. Here are found the major cultural, economic, and political institutions: faculties of the University, museums, the Orthodox Cathedral (*Saborna Crkva*), the Patriarch's Palace (*Patrijaršija*), the Church of St. Mark, the National Theater, the Parliament (*Skupština*), the Headquarters of the Communist Party of Yugoslavia, the former Royal Palace, major hotels, depart-

---

[43]For further general historical material regarding Belgrade, see Marić, Dinić, Samadžić, Nikolić, and Jovanović (1954), Paunović (1968), and Popović (1964). Šolajić (1954) is an excellent source regarding the military history of Belgrade. Regarding the city during the Middle Ages, refer to Kalić-Mijušković (1967). For a description of Belgrade during the nineteenth century, see Andrić *et al.* (1967) and Perić (1967). Perić's work consists of a collection of translations of the accounts of foreign travelers in Belgrade during the nineteenth century.

TABLE 9

Geographic Divisions of Belgrade

Administrative Divisions (opštine)[a]

1. Cukarica	6. Voždovac
2. Novi Beograd	7. Vračar
3. Palilula	8. Zemun
4. Savski Venac	9. Zvezdara
5. Stari Grad	

Popularly designated areas within Belgrade proper

10. Banovo Brdo	20. Košutnjak
11. Bulbulder	21. Kotež Neimar
12. Čalije	22. Lekino Brdo
13. Čubura	23. Marinkova Bara
14. Dedinje	24. Senjak
15. Dorćol	25. Stari Djeram
16. Dušanovac	26. Šumice
17. Hadži Popovac	27. Terazija
18. Kalemegdan	28. Topčidersko Brdo
19. Konjarnik	

Semirural areas closely tied to the city

29. Banjica	33. Rakovica
30. Kanarevo Brdo	34. Višnjica
31. Krnjača	35. Zarkovo
32. Mokri Lug	

Satellite urban communities

36. Novi Beograd[b]   37. Bežanija
38. Pančevo (located in the Banat area of the Vojvodina)[b]
39. Zemun (until 1918 part of Austro-Hungary; located immediately across the Sava River from Belgrade

---

[a]At present Yugoslavia is divided into *opštine* (communes) which comprise the level of administration under the republic. Formerly there was an intermediate unit known as the *srez* (an approximate equivalent of the American county which has now been abolished. Belgrade is a so-called *multicommunal city* in that it contains all of, or parts of, 9 of the 14 *opštine* of the former *srez* of Belgrade.

[b]Novi Beograd, Pančevo, and Zemun are also *opštine*. Pančevo is not regarded as part of Belgrade, but is economically and culturally tied to the capital (though located some 18 kilometers to the east).

ment stores brimming with consumer goods, boutiques, and restaurants.

The heart of the city mirrors the eclectic taste of Serbian builders and architects. The Cathedral, completed in 1854, is the product of renaissance and baroque inspirations forced into a Byzantine mold; the National Theater and the Royal Palace display the combination of Italian and Gothic styles; while the still incomplete Church of St. Mark, looming above Tašmajdan Park with its modern sports center and swimming pool, is a return to the indigenous Serbo-Byzantine past. Dwarfed by monumental structures of a later age, remnants of the oriental past persist here and there: the Bath of Prince Miloš (*Amam Kneza Miloša*) and the Cafe Question Mark (*Kafana Kod Znaka Pitanja*), both constructed in the early nineteenth century, closely follow Turkish tastes.

The core of the city, often simply referred to as *the center*, is a magnet for the capital's populace. The vitality and extent of life and movement on the streets is striking to Americans unfamiliar with Mediterranean culture. By day, crowds jam the sidewalks from early morning; some window-shop, gazing at the multiplicity of still novel consumer goods given prominent display in the show windows; others pause to leisurely greet friends, and often linger long in conversation, unaware of the passage of time and caring little to hurry on; the ubiquitous cafes and garden restaurants are filled to capacity with men sipping Turkish coffee, and one puzzles: when, where, and by whom is the society's work carried on? Only in the midafternoon is there a hiatus of activity. This is a time reserved by tradition for the family, the major meal of the day (*ručak*), and the declining custom of the siesta.

By the early evening hours the tempo has resumed its former intensity. It is along the Street of Prince Michael (*Knez Mihailova Ulica*) that the throngs are densest, since it is here that the institution of the daily promenade is observed. In Serbia it bears the name *korzo* or *štafeta*, but differs in little else from its counterparts in Greece, Spain, Italy, or Latin America. The thoroughfare is closed to vehicular traffic, and groups of well-dressed young people stroll, to all appearances aimlessly, back and forth along the six blocks dedicated to this activity. Young men sporting white shirts, ties, often modish suits, and shoes polished to a mirror finish walk arm-in-arm eyeing, with seemingly casual disinterest, the girls, who circulate, for the most part, in groups of their

"The city now becomes the domain of the carouser, a man's world populated by Gypsy musicians . . ."

own sex.[44] In other parts of the city, variants of this same activity take place, but on a smaller scale and with fewer pretensions to elegance and contemporaneity.

As night draws on, the streets gradually empty of the dense crowds, since most must prepare for the work day, which commences at 6:00 A.M. in the summer, and an hour, sometimes two, later in the winter months. The city now becomes the domain of the carouser, a man's world populated by Gypsy musicians, waiters, bar girls and prostitutes, cab drivers, and drunks. Cabarets featuring inept stripteasers, often badly performed Western popular hits, and nightclub comics vie with smoke-filled cellars offering regional folk music, skewered Middle Eastern roasted meats served with mounds of chopped raw unions and red pepper relish (*ajvar*), and the native plum brandy (*šljivovica*).

---

[44]Traditional patterns of sexual segregation apply to the evening promenade. Males outnumber females overwhelmingly. On one occasion during the *štafeta* I counted 11 times as many males as females. On the basis of numerous observations I would conclude that the general composition of the *korzo* consists of the following (in order of frequency): (1) pairs or groups of young males; (2) single males; (3) groups or pairs of females; (4) heterosexual couples or mixed groups; (5) couples consisting of a young female (15–30 years old) and an older woman; (6) single girls (quite rare).

The constant roar of motor traffic, the shiny facades of new construction, and the predominantly Western dress of pedestrians cannot hide the fact that, even here at the very pivot of the contemporary city, the past perceptively impinges on the present, and the countryside on the urban milieu. The heritage of poverty and the East is clearly visible in the Gypsy beggar accosting passersby with outstretched palm soliciting *bakšiš* (alms). Self-service cafeterias stand but a few doors from cafes of the old school, with their smoking charcoal braziers and sizzling kabobs. Oriental sweetshops dispense delicacies whose exotic names echo of the Levant: *rahat-lokum, ćeten-alva,* and *baklava.* Peasant women, unselfconscious in their many petticoats, babushkas, and rubber moccasins, walk side by side with their men in country pants cut tight below the knee in the style of riding britches. Villagers, perhaps seeking a bit of diverison and novelty after the market, linger in the city, gazing in shop windows at television sets, radios, ready-made shoes, and plastic kitchenware. The tourist or foreigner, however, unacquainted with the culture and history of Serbia and remaining close to the reassuring universality of modern hotels, following familiar paths to museums, department stores, and hygienic-appearing eating establishments, will perhaps leave Belgrade unaware of the delight of discovering its traditional Balkan substructure.

In many ways, the wide avenue of the Boulevard of the Revolution (*Bulevar Revolucije*) typifies the several contrasting faces of the city. This major artery runs from the capital's nucleus to its outskirts, thence out into the countryside along the Danube to the ancient fortress city of Smederevo with its decaying ramparts standing guard on the river banks since 1430. The Boulevard of the Revolution commences at the modernistic Square of Marx and Engels constructed in 1956, and passes the Parliament, St. Mark's Church, the massive stone Central Post Office, Belgrade's most exclusive hotel (the Metropol), faculties of the University and well-tended parks. Within a dozen or so blocks the street quickly changes its aspect; the imposing structures of government and academia give way to small shops, dilapidated single-storied buildings of Balkan line, shabby coffeehouses, working-class restaurants and cafes, and the tiny workshops of independent craftsmen. The peeling ochre facades of poorly maintained stucco

"A focus of activity is the Stari Djeram open market . . ." Peasant woman from Banatsko Novo Selo at the *pijaca*

walls provide relief from the grayness and formalism of the central district. A focus of activity is the Stari Djeram open market, one of Belgrade's many at which the majority of the city's housewives secure their daily nutritional needs, dealing directly with independent peasant producers as well as with the numerous retail outlets of agricultural cooperatives and socialist enterprises also found here. National dress appears more frequently among those passing along the broad sidewalks, and those in modern attire are less aware of the nuances of Western styles. Quiet peripheral streets are frequently paved with large, rounded Turkish cobblestones, and are bordered by brick or masonry walls which partially obscure modest tile-roofed homes with their pleasant gardens filled with dahlias, acacia, and potted lemons and geraniums. In true southern fashion, terraces, open porches, and balconies are transformed into thickets of greenery by much-tended tubs of luxuriant shrubs and flowers.

Toward the outskirts, settlement becomes sparser, and houses of an increasingly peasant type predominate, though occasional spires of high-rise apartments sound an incongruous note. Side streets and alleyways are often unpaved, and farm animals, horse-drawn peasant carts, and cultivated plots are much in evidence. The city's periphery is, in fact, partially composed of villages which have been surrounded by the expanding urban complex, but which still function to a degree as agrarian social and economic entities, semirural enclaves in contemporary Belgrade.[45]

The clash of old and new is manifest in most aspects of the city. Modern economic life is exemplified by cooperative enterprises[46] belonging to the "public" or "socialist sector": factories, construction companies, supermarkets, department stores, wholesale distributors, and agencies and services of many types. Traditional economic activities persist, for the most part, in the "private sector," that is, in the realm of the small entrepreneur. The free peasant market system is but one example. Independent craftsmen, often specializing in trades of preindustrial or Turkish origin (bakers, quiltmakers, candlemakers, silversmiths, shoemakers, and many others), pursue their trades under conditions which would be considered primitive, inefficient, and intolerable by Western standards. A shoemaker, for example, may work in a shop no larger than a closet, perhaps 4 feet wide and 6 feet deep. The only light is provided by single bulb of low wattage suspended from the ceiling, and the rays of sun that penetrate during warm weather when the door or shutters may remain open. He works seated on the floor or on a low stool surrounded by his meager materials and limited assortment of hand tools. During the severe continental winter, heat is provided by a tiny charcoal brazier. Door-to-door peddlers are also a common sight

[45]For example, Višnjica, which lies but a 10-minute walk from Karaburma along a dirt road, is an almost totally peasant and rural community in its general features, though many of its inhabitants are employed in Belgrade industry.

[46]Regarding the socialist firm and "worker self-management," see Ward (1965).

"Traditional economic activities persist . . ." Gypsy woman selling rugbeaters and wooden kitchen utensils at the Kalenić market place.

in Belgrade: vendors of cheese, eggs, wine, spirits (*rakija*), feathers, and handicrafts. As is frequently the case in underdeveloped or developing nations, economic necessity has forced many to acquire marginally rewarding occupations as a means of survival: itinerant musicians, knife and scissor sharpeners, umbrella repairmen, shoeshine men, ragpickers, and street merchants dealing in lottery tickets, patent medicines, postcards, or snacks such as roasted ears of corn or chestnuts. *Šiptar* (Albanian Moslem) porters and odd-job men in once-white felt skullcaps pass the time of day on street corners waiting for employment.[47] Many goods and much

[47]The ethnic division of labor in Belgrade is evident though not rigid. Gypsies tend to work as musicians, metalworkers, smiths, shoeshine boys, ragpickers, and small-scale ambulant merchants. Albanians find employment as porters, odd-job men, and construction workers. Macedonians and Serbs from southern Serbia also show a predilection for work in the heavy construction industry. Peasant girls from the Slovak minority in Vojvodina provide a large part of Belgrade's domestic help.

produce are still transported on foot, in pushcarts, or by three-wheeled vehicles converted from bicycles. Most independent craftsmen possess no personal means of transportation, and often must send their materials in this manner to the site of their work. Plumbers, carpenters, or electricians frequently so lack equipment that they can carry their entire selection of tools in a single leather briefcase.

Ritual life, too, reflects the dichotomy between the past and present. In contrast to the yearly calendar of secular celebrations marking milestones in the growth of the new socialist state (May Day, the Day of the Republic, etc.), religious holidays provide an opportunity to observe the vigor of traditional Serbian culture in an urban setting. The *slava* (celebration of the patron saint) of the little Orthodox Church of the Presentation (*Crkva Vavedenja*) in Topčider Park on July 12, the Day of Saints Peter and Paul, is an event at which city and country custom stand side by side. On this occasion, smartly dressed Belgradians rub shoulders with

Popular Belgrade Gypsy musician "Paganini" sings into the sound box of his violin.

peasants in regional folk costume. The festival is held in the same manner as a village or small-town *sabor* (church fair). Following Holy Liturgy in the morning, the grounds quickly fill with celebrants. Merchants, for the most part Gypsies, lay their wares on the grass while others attract players to simple games of chance. Petty entrepreneurs sell warm beer and soft drinks from wooden barrels of tepid water. Musicians gather with accordions, bass fiddles, violins, clarinets, and trumpets. Circles form, and the *kolo*, a line dance of endless variants, commences. The participants are principally recent arrivals from the village, peasants from the environs of Belgrade, or visiting rural kin on a sojourn in the city. The more urbanized and sophisticated remain aloof on the sidelines, enjoying the festivities with a feigned air of bored detachment. The Serbian (not the Yugoslav) red, white, and blue tricolor, fluttering from the facade of the church, points to the highly national and regional character of this observance.

It is not surprising that Belgradians often comment that their city is in reality a "big village." Moreover, many express the feeling that Serbia somehow lies outside the sphere of "civilization." They speak of "going to Europe," and an elderly former aristocrat once told me: "You are blessed to live in the cultured world" (*Blago vama što živite u kulturnom svetu*). "Civilization" and "the cultured world" do not refer to political ideologies, but rather to ideas regarding life styles, and proximity to the main currents of world trends. One constantly encounters small, but telling, reminders that this is not the West, but rather some half-way station between Europe and the East, between the past and present. Within five blocks of the National Theater the early morning hours are punctuated by the crow of roosters , and on the city streets one may be approached by a peasant in homespun dress offering a freshly slaughtered suckling pig which he has produced tail-first from a battered suitcase. Past display windows exhibiting the fruits of industry, I watched a Gypsy wedding party serpentine along the street, dancing to the asymmetrical shifting rhythms of the *tapan* (a large skin-covered drum) and *zurla* (a double-reed, oboelike instrument common throughout the Middle East). More contemporary and affluent couples speed to their wedding festivities in Fiats bedecked with plastic flowers and towels (the towels are tied on the hood just under the windshield) in the same manner that horse-drawn fiacres are decorated for village weddings (cf. Halpern, 1958, p. 193).

If one were to seek a meeting place of all strata of Belgrade society, a place where contrasts were most acute, the railroad station would probably best fulfill this requirement. This massive neoclassical structure and the adjoining contemporary, recently constructed bus depot provide the principal funnels through which rural elements enter the city and urbanites return to visit village kin. It is here that country girls commence their careers as prostitutes, and those who have failed to acclimatize or prosper in the city take their last look at Belgrade. On the waiting platforms every imaginable combination of modern dress and national costume can be seen. Peasants sit cross-legged on the ground eating their modest supper of bread, tomatoes, cucumbers, yogurt, and brandy. Young "sophisticates" stand stiffly in tapered pants and pointed shoes of Italian cut waiting for the train that will take

"More contemporary and affluent couples speed to their wedding festivities in Fiats bedecked with plastic flowers and towels in the same manner that fiacres are decorated for village weddings."

them to visit parents or kin in remote villages in southern Serbia or Macedonia. A youth, in ready-made clothes, guides his old father in a fez and his mother in *dimije* (Moslem pantaloons) to the ticket window to start them on their trip home to a village high in the forested mountains of Bosnia.

While the incongruities and contrasts typical of developing nations are everywhere evident in the external life of Belgrade, it is my assumption that they will be mirrored to an even greater degree in the individual, who, as the primary agent of change, must experience and resolve the conflicts inherent in the rapid transition of his society. In this respect his basic beliefs, values, and modes of behavior will reflect his own and his country's intermediacy between the preindustrial and the modern world. Moreover, the contemporary Serb is also the sum total of his past, the product of those opposing forces and philosophies that have shaped his nation. Thus, the description of his traditional institutions and history have been a necessary preface to the interpretation of his role in the process of industrialization and urbanization.

CHAPTER IV

RURAL–URBAN MIGRATION IN SERBIA: MOTIVATION AND PROCESS

Introduction

During the centuries of Moslem occupation there had been some modest migration by the Serbs away from the villages to the cities and towns. With the defeat and withdrawal of the Turks the pace of urbanization quickened slightly. The Ottomans, who had previously determined and dominated the character of urban life, left behind them a vacuum that was filled by the indigenous population. However, the magnitude of urban growth was greatly restricted by the traditional nature of the economy and the lack of an industrial base.

The massive shifts in the Yugoslav population that have taken place since the close of the Second World War may be directly related to the rapid expansion of industry, construction, services, and the bureaucracy. A causal relationship can be drawn between the sharp increase in the number of new work positions outside of agriculture created by the economic transformation of the society, and the large-scale rural–urban migration that has occurred during the last quarter of a century. At one time a move to the city was undoubtedly considered exceptional behavior by village norms, and only a few were able to escape into the priesthood, law, commerce, or the trades. In contrast, the postwar period has been one in which the abandonment of the countryside has become feasible for such large numbers that this choice is now regarded as one of the anticipated alternatives of peasant life. It is doubtful that any village in Yugoslavia has not contributed some of its members to the expanding urban milieu. Moreover, many rural communities have lost a significant proportion of their young work force, and in extreme cases, most often in the agriculturally unproductive Dinaric regions of western Yugoslavia, some villages have been left populated almost entirely by the aged.

In this chapter I propose to examine the exodus from the Yugoslav countryside from the standpoint of its motivative stimuli, and to view the migratory process in its spatial and chronological dimensions. Generalizations will be drawn from the analysis of the case histories of the migrants themselves. The validity of an approach to the study of social mobility focusing on the individual is pointed out by Hammel (1969, p. 90) in his study of workers employed by four large Belgrade enterprises. Though he cites the obvious relationship between fluctuations in the economic system and occupational mobility, he cautions that we should not ignore the role of the individual in the social drama of mobility, and that he is only attempting to point out "the importance of the stage setting and the script."

Motivative Factors in Migration

While general economic, social, and political conditions may explain migration as a mass phenomenon within a specific geographic and historical context, the analysis of individual cases reveals a complex interplay of determining variables that are both numerous and diverse. Several levels of analysis are suggested, and in terms of focus these can be viewed as a continuum whose polarities range from the general socioeconomic characteristics of the society as a whole to those of the individual, who acts as the ultimate locus of change. Each person is affected to an increasing degree of specificity by the salient features and history of his nation, region, and village. Moreover, his potentialities are further delineated by accident of birth and that particular chain of events which constitutes his life history. Similarly, the individual's freedom of choice is limited not only by the actual alternatives open to him but also by his ability to perceive them. Thus, the examination of the decision-making process must address itself to the nature of subjective states and judgments as well as to an assessment of objective reality.

Motivating factors in migration may be explained as a reaction to what are conceived of as unfavorable existing conditions contrasted with projections regarding potential rewards resulting from spatial mobility. Moreover, the possible advantages of migration and optimistic images of the urban milieu must outweigh the strength of traditional social ties, the attachment to the predictable and familiar, and the often tenuous security of the land. The inducements of city life must also overcome fears and insecurities regarding an unfamiliar environment in which the peasant will occupy, at least initially, a position of relatively low status.

Each village or town consists of a specific socioeconomic environment having a characteristic image in the eyes of its inhabitants. At this level of analysis a number of negative characteristics can be abstracted from the narratives of migrant informants. The rural community is frequently portrayed in terms of its disadvantageous economic situation, and the same complaints are voiced repeatedly: the poor quality and unproductivity of the land; idleness outside of peak agricultural periods; lack of employment opportunities in fields other than agriculture; the low monetary reward for produce; exclusion from fringe benefits general in other branches of the economy (retirement income, disability insurance, and full medical coverage); and fluctuations in and unpredictability of income. Dissatisfaction with the noneconomic aspects of village life is stressed to an equal degree. Tortuous, unimproved roads and trails make access to markets and regional urban centers difficult, and perhaps more significantly, contribute to a general sense of isolation. In the same manner, distance from important political and cultural foci weakens the feeling of participation in national life. The lack of facilities and services also creates a sense of alienation from the contemporary world. Some Yugoslav villages may have as few as 50 inhabitants. These are especially common in the Dinaric regions of the west, and often simply consist of a number of dispersed farmsteads scattered over a wide geographic area. These may lack such basic facilities as a school, a church or mosque, or a general store. Larger peasant communities may boast a retail outlet, a meeting hall (*dom*), and a religious center, yet have only a 4-year educational institution. Even villages and provincial towns with populations numbering in the thousands frequently do not provide education beyond the eighth grade. The restrictive nature of such communities, the lack of educational and employment opportunities, limited diversions, and primitive living conditions, drive many villagers to seek a more varied, stimulating, and comfortable environment. Additionally, many complain of the low level of anonymity, the highly personalized social controls, and the narrow latitude for behavior and self-expression.

The following examples illustrate the manner in which informants express negative evaluations of their native villages.

> *My village is isolated, and though we are only 13 kilometers from the city of Leskovac, it might as well be 100. There is no good road and one must walk a good part of the way. There is really nothing good in my village. In the summer one kills himself with work, and in the winter there is nothing to do.*

> *Our village has only one main crop, tobacco; if it fails we all suffer.*

> *I was born in a miserable, impoverished village in Montenegro. The land is poor—we are surrounded by naked stone. One lives as best he can.*

> *It is monotonous in the village—one can rest too much. But the worst thing is the gossip.*

The soil in our village is fourth class. For the most part we eat only beans, corn, and peppers. The whole family sleeps in one room on straw.

*In the village one has no life of his own. People know your business and news travels fast. We call this the **village telephone**.*

Emigration from the village may also be seen as stemming from economic factors specific to given individuals and families. Though differences in wealth are not great, and even the most affluent are limited to a modest standard of living, on the bottom of the scale a number find themselves living at a bare subsistence level. Rural poverty can often be attributed to insufficient land resources, either in absolute terms or in relation to family size and the number of possible inheritors. Rural holdings vary in regard to their quality, the degree of fragmentation, and the geographic dispersal of cultivable plots. Households also differ as to the size of their herds and flocks, the extent and nature of agricultural equipment and facilities, and the quality and spaciousness of housing. Moreover, families demonstrate considerable variation in their skill in management and utilization of available resources. The case of Panto provides an illustration of poverty as a prime motivator for migration to the city:

I was the youngest of three brothers and two sisters. In my grandfather's time there had been scarcely enough land to support the family. When he died, the holdings were divided among my father and his two brothers. Each received so little it hardly mattered. Not only that, the quality of our land was poor, we had little stock, and the house was falling into ruins. Since my two brothers were married with children, there was nothing for me to do but leave and let them work my share.

Household composition and the quality of interpersonal relations within the family are significant variables related to migration. For instance, the inability of the wives of coinheriting brothers to live amicably under the same roof can result in the division of commonly held property, or in the emigration of one or more of the concerned nuclear families. Hammel (1968, p. 15) has called attention to this problem as a contributory factor to the fission of the traditional South Slav *zadruga*, where inmarrying wives provided pivotal points for its dissolution. Milorad, who had migrated from a village in Šumadija 18 years ago, characterized this phenomenon in terms of his own experience:

> *My wife, three children, and I lived in a* zadruga *with my brother, his wife, and two children. We did not have enough land, but what was worse, we argued, especially the women. So I gave my holdings to my brother and came to Belgrade. I think living in a* **zadruga** *is the greatest cause of quarrels, and even murder, in Serbia.*

The death of a close kin who provided a focus for family cohesion may act as an impetus for the abandonment of the village. Such an event can bring to a head the problem of partitive inheritance, and in the case of grandsons the situation may be further complicated by differential rights to the patrimony.[1] Moreover, among the Serbs, loyalties and emotional attachments are more intense to kin than they are to specific localities or communities. The example of Nule is illustrative of this tendency:

> *We did not have a large family, and my uncles and aunts had long ago died. When my mother and father passed away, there was nothing more to hold me in the village, so I sold the land and set off for Belgrade.*

Alienation on the part of the individual due to what are perceived as highly personalized and excessive rural social controls can account for a number of instances of migration. This is particularly true in the case of women, who are typically allowed less freedom of public behavior in traditional Serbian society, which has highly differentiated sex-role expectations (cf. Hammel, 1967; Simić, 1969). For example, a Yugoslav criminologist commented that the rural origins of the majority of Belgrade prostitutes[2] can be accounted for by the fact that these girls have

---

[1]When land is divided among grandsons, each receives an equal part of what would have been his father's share. First cousins may thus receive unequal shares, determined by the number of inheriting brothers of each.

[2]Though there are no figures available for Belgrade, a study of 146 Zagreb prostitutes by Marković (1965) showed that 54.55% were born in the village; 25% were born in provincial towns of cities; and only 20.45% were from Zagreb by birth.

drifted into the city because of conflicts with village norms. In his words, "There is no place in the village for a girl with an illegitimate child. It reflects not only on her, but on the entire household and extended family."

In the evaluation of rural life migrants frequently expressed generalized emotional states stemming from feelings of non-specific dissatisfaction. These were described in terms of "boredom," "futility," "frustration," or "hopelessness." Similarly, the village was sometimes stereotyped as "bad," "miserable," "un-cultured," or "backward." As one informant simply put it, "that life kills a man" (*taj život ubije čoveka*).

Complementing such negative views of rural life were positive attitudes and expectations regarding the urban experience. These too were frequently phrased in abstract terms such as "ambition," "excitement," "adventure," or "culture" (in Yugoslav popular usage *kultura* most often bears the connotation of a comfortable and contemporary life style).

Exposure to such ideas may be vicarious or direct. On a general level one cannot ignore the tremendous influence of the mass media, which in the postwar years has reached even the most remote villages in the form of radio, and in many cases television. Through the media a multitude of impressions has been disseminated regarding the urban milieu. In particular, a desire has been created for greater participation in modern life through the cash economy. In this respect peasant households are anxious to have some of their members employed outside of agriculture in order to obtain manufactured goods and a pre-dictable income. The case studies indicate that, indeed, migrants often fulfill these expectations.

Probably the most significant indirect contact with the city is through the experiences of kin or covillagers who have taken up residence in an urban center. By means of such relationships it is possible not only to judge the possibilities of success in migra-tion, but also to be assured of a helping hand during the difficult period of settlement and adjustment in an unfamiliar environ-ment. Nikola, who had recently arrived in Belgrade, recounted the following.

The land couldn't produce enough for all of us but I didn't know what to do. A neighbor who had been working in Belgrade arrived one day to visit kin in the village. He encouraged me to return to the city with him, so I decided to try my luck.

Direct experience outside the village also stimulates a desire for change. Military service, which is almost universal in Yugoslavia, provides an important source of exposure to new ideas. Recruits are customarily assigned to a region distant from their homes, and few complete their obligation without some contact with urban life. Moreover, within the military a young man can receive further education or become proficient in a craft or other occupational specialty. For instance, Radenko, who migrated to Belgrade after completing his army service, attributes his desire for mobility to "the many books I found available in camp." Another informant stated that the army was the "turning point" in his life, and while serving in the Bosnian industrial city of Banja Luka he was exposed to "another kind of existence."

Education must be reckoned as a major factor in migration. Not only is a general desire for increased participation in the world outside the village created, but skills are often acquired which either cannot be practiced in the countryside, or which can be applied with greater rewards elsewhere. I have already noted that many villages and provincial towns do not possess facilities for advanced education or specialized training. Thus, those who desire schooling beyond the eighth grade must reside at least temporarily outside their birthplaces in larger population centers. Many who do so never again return to live permanently in their native communities. For instance, Mira was sent by her parents to live with a paternal aunt in Belgrade so that she could attend secondary school. She found life in the city "more interesting," and decided to remain permanently in the capital. In a somewhat different case, Radovan, who had finished four grades in the village, was sent by his parents to reside in a nearby provincial town to attend trade school. However, he was unable to finish the course of study because of the family's poverty. Though he was forced to return home, the desire to eventually take up life in the city was stimulated by the experience.

Seasonal or temporary labor in the city provides another mode of exposure to urban life. A number of rural areas in southern Serbia and Macedonia have a tradition of migrant labor (*pe-*

čalbarstvo), and many peasant boys catch their first glimpse of the city in this manner. Such was the case of Mile, who came to Belgrade as an unskilled worker on a construction project. He lived in a company barracks on the city outskirts until the completion of the job. Though he then returned to his village, a few years later he set off to take up permanent residence in the capital.

Continuing close contact between rural and urban kin after migration provides villagers with an opportunity to visit the city. Visiting patterns between rural and urban family branches are frequently intense. The impact of such exposure is clear. For example, Zora decided to remain in Belgrade after a summer visit with a sister who had migrated several years earlier. As she explained

> *After staying in the city with my sister I dreaded returning to our village. Before I saw Belgrade I had no idea how monotonous and difficult my life in the countryside was.*

Regardless of the mode of exposure to urban ideas, the images and expectations are quite consistent with all informants. Opportunities for greater comfort, better employment, and a more stimulating life style are the most frequently stated attributes of the Belgrade milieu. There is a conviction that residence in the nation's capital and employment outside of agriculture are more prestigious than the life of a peasant. Moreover, even if an individual does not experience outstanding success in the city, his children can enjoy the many advantages lacking in the rural community, the most important of which are educational and occupational mobility.

It should be noted that migration to Belgrade has been from provincial towns and cities as well as from the village. Nonrural migration differs somewhat in terms of its motivating stimuli in that problems associated with an agricultural life are not a consideration (e.g., partitive inheritance, unpredictable income). Paramount is concern for increased vertical mobility and participation in a more heterogeneous cultural and social environment. Moreover, impetus for migration from provincial urban centers tends to take the form of a single explicit purpose, such as the attainment of a university education or the seeking of a financially more rewarding job. Small-town and urban migrants also tend to arrive in the city armed with higher qualifications and skills than their rural counterparts, and need not as frequently begin life in the capital at the bottom of the socioeconomic ladder. For the skilled worker, the city offers a wider spectrum of possible employment; for the bureaucrat, a more broadly based hierarchical pyramid for advancement; and for the entrepreneur, an extensive and potentially more affluent clientele.

Spatial and Chronological Dimensions of Migration

Though the transfer of residence from village to city may consist of a single move by an individual, most frequently the spatial and chronological dimensions of migration exhibit a more complex structure. Rural–urban mobility generally involves a number of members of a family or kin group, and a process often spanning several generations. There may be one or more hiatuses between the point of departure and that of culmination. While it is relatively easy to discern the beginning of migration for a given family, it is difficult to anticipate its completion.

The spatial aspects of migration exhibit a number of simple variations. The two most common patterns are a direct move from the native village to Belgrade, or migration to the capital with intermediate residence in a provincial town near one's place of birth.

Hammel (1969b, p. 83) comments that provincial industry in Yugoslavia has drawn on peasant labor surplus before urban industry. The tendency to first accept employment in the town or city nearest to one's home can be explained not only in terms of the availability of positions but also as the result of personal preference. With a job near the village it is possible to enjoy the emotional and material security of remaining in a familiar environment, and at the same time to develop skills and gain experience outside of agriculture. Thus, armed with at least minimal qualifications it is possible to proceed to Belgrade with somewhat greater assurance of success. For others, the provinces become a final destination. For example, an urban informant who had migrated from a village some years ago supplied a genealogy consisting of 142 living consanguine and affinal kin, 39 of whom reside in Belgrade while 42 live in the three provincial towns nearest their cluster of native villages.[3] It is, of course, impossible to predict how many of these 42 will continue on to the capital, or how many of their children will do likewise.

Less frequently the migratory pattern involves movement to a second, often larger or richer, village before settlement in Belgrade. These cases can be explained in terms of a number of causes and motivations. For example, following the war, rich agricultural lands in the Vojvodina were confiscated from the German minority (*Volksdeutsch*) and other large landholders, and redistributed to peasants from unproductive areas and to Serbs who had fled during the war from the persecution of the pro-Nazi Independent State of Croatia (*Nezavisna Država Hrvatska*). More idiosyncratic reasons include, among others, the possibility of an advantageous marriage to an inheriting daughter; the presence in the richer community of kin or affines who are already well established; the purchase of land; or the opportunity to practice a craft or trade. In some instances, after an initial move to a second village or provincial town, the migrant returns to his original home for a period of months or even years before proceeding to Belgrade.

Family members only occasionally reach the city as a group. The sexual dichotomy is especially evident in the migratory process. Brothers generally precede sisters, and husbands establish a base in the city sometimes years before they are joined by wives and children. In one case, an informant has lived in Belgrade for almost eight years, and still maintains his wife and six children in a village in southern Serbia. Men who follow this pattern express

[3]The genealogy shows the following total distribution of residence. Belgrade and its environs (including Zemun, New Belgrade, and Železnik) are inhabited by 39; most of the rest live either in provincial towns near the cluster of native villages, including Gornji Milanovac (24), Takovo (13), and Čačak (5); or in the native villages themselves: Šarani (16); Bešići (8); Vrnčani (9); Sinoševići (5); Veroleči (3); Crnuće (2); Kalimanići (2); Lozanj (2); Semedraž (2); and Grabovica (1). Of the remaining 11 persons, 7 reside in more distant parts of the Serbian Republic (4 in Kosovska Mitrovica and 3 in the region of Banat in Vojvodina), while only one nuclear family of 4 members resides outside of Serbia in the Bosnian town of Doboj. In this case the husband, who is a consanguine kin of the informant, is an army officer stationed in Bosnia. Genealogical material from other kin groups in the sample indicates very similar migratory patterns and verifies the tendency for spatial mobility to generally observe ethnic boundaries.

little or no anxiety about their wives since these women remain safely in the bosom of kin who "watch over their welfare." Also, there are no cultural expectations regarding sexual fidelity on the part of the male, and by contributing financially to the family he is fulfilling his most basic role. Although the migration of a wife before a husband appears extremely rare,[4] there are some instances in which sisters arrive in the city before their brothers. This is especially common where higher education is a motivative factor, and in such cases the women usually take up residence with some kin or affine who can offer aid and, most important, security. Those who arrive in the city without the assurance of such "protection" risk severe criticism in their villages as well as being regarded as "fair game" for aggressive, predatory, urban males.

It is not surprising, in the light of the strong elements of family and kinship corporacy in Serbian social organization, that migration is seldom an entirely individual matter. The first member of a family to migrate is not likely to be the last, and in most cases he will aid other kin to follow in his footsteps. Nor does such responsibility end in the migrating generation, but also falls to succeeding generations born in the city. In many ways, the urban household can be viewed as an extension of the village family, as a base for further expansion from the land.

The example of the Pavlović family illustrates the manner in which migration is a continuing process, often spanning several generations, and how the corporate family ideology is reflected in mutual aid as an aspect of rural–urban mobility:

> *I was born in a village near the town of Paraćin. I am the youngest of three sisters and two brothers. My parents were peasants, but sold the land and settled in Parać shotly before the last war. We remained very poor, and there were few opportunities in such a small place. After the war my oldest brother, Milan, migrated to Belgrade. He arrived without a dinar in his pocket but somehow succeeded. After a year he brought his wife and two children to the capital. As he prospered he brought each of us to the city, and one by one got us through school and settled. He is really someone*

---

[4]No single case occurred in the sample except where the marriage had taken place after migration.

to be proud of! My husband and I in our turn are now aiding other kin to come and settle in Belgrade. We almost always have someone from the provinces staying with us.

Case Studies

In some cases single motivating stimuli may be pointed out as the primary cause, or as vastly more significant than other factors in migration. More commonly, decisions are formulated on the basis of an individual's entire life sequence and as the result of a multitude of considerations. While the specification of discrete motivative elements has a value for generalization, analysis, and comparison, their role is somewhat distorted when viewed outside of the contexts in which they appear. The following case studies are illustrative of the field material and may be taken as typical of the responses of rural migrants in Belgrade, though they do not encompass the entire range of the data collected.

*I was born in the village of Kalimanići near Gornji Malanovac. There are about 400 people in my village. My family was neither rich nor poor, just about like everyone else. Since it was not far, my parents sent me to school in Gornji Milanovac, where I completed the ninth grade. The first chance I had to glimpse the outside world was in 1930, when I was stationed in the infantry in Zagreb. I could see that people in the city lived more comfortable lives than we did in the countryside. My mother died in 1932 shortly after my return from the army. My father lived until 1941. Upon his death my brother and I received 6 hectares [1 hectare equals 2.471 acres] of unproductive land, which we worked together. According to our custom, my sister received no inheritance in land but only a dowry of household goods. My brother, Dragan, had a wife and several children, and when I chose a bride from a nearby village I brought her home to live with us in a **zadruga**. My three children were all born in the village. We had a very hard time making a go of it. There were too many people for the land to support. For awhile I worked in the village cooperative, but this job didn't last long. I was already 42 years old when I decided to try my luck in the city. I sold part of my share of the land to the neighbors, and the rest to my brother. I was lucky when I arrived in Belgrade,* *and found a job right away. It took a year to bring my family to the city because I could not find adequate housing. I look back on my life in the village as a difficult one. I am a good worker, and I think what bothered me most of all was the fact that I could find no productive way to use my time during the winter when there was nothing to do in the fields.*

I was born in a Serbian village in the Gorski Kotar region of Croatia. My parents were poor peasants, and if we had remained on the land, my mother and father would have had a difficult time supporting my brother and us three girls. But fate willed otherwise. I was only 3 years old when we had to flee for our lives. The **ustaša** [pro-Nazi terrorists] *came into our village and killed many Serbian peasants, but somehow we managed to hide and save ourselves. We headed directly for Belgrade, where we could be safe among our own people. After the war we decided that life was more comfortable in the city, so we gave our land to those relatives that had survived, because they were impoverished and needed it to live.*

My village of Gradište [in southern Serbia near Leskovac] *is very poor, primitive, and isolated. I was the youngest boy in a family of four brothers and two sisters. One of my brothers and my sister were killed during the war. We were ordinary peasants and worked the land. Before the war I finished 4 years of elementary school, which was all our village offered. My first experience in the outside world was when I was 18 and served in the army on the Adriatic Coast in Dalmatia and Montenegro. Perhaps it was then that I realized that I no longer wanted to live in the village. I could see no future there. When I got out of the army I wandered around Yugoslavia working at this and that. After seeing many places, I decided that Belgrade was the best place for me. It was the biggest city and also located in Serbia not too far from my home. My two brothers had already gone into industry, and when my father died in 1962 we sold most of our land to the village cooperative. My mother is still in Gradište and living in our houe on the small parcel of land that we kept. When I decided to get married, I went back to the village and took the daughter of our nearest neighbor. She stayed in Gradište with my mother for the first 5 years of our marriage and both of our children were born there. When I finally found a decent place to live, I brought them to Belgrade. There is really nothing in our village, during the summer one kills himself with work, and in the winter there is nothing to do.*

I have had a difficult life. I was born in an impoverished village near Petrovići in Montegnegro. The land was poor, good only for raising goats. When I was a young girl my father died and my mother and I were left alone. It is a miracle how the two of us managed to live. If it were not for the help of my father's kin, who pitched in with the work and gave us food, I think we would have starved to death. The war came and there was fighting all around us. We fled to Priština, where my father had a distant relative who took us in. We lived hand to mouth, and somehow I was able to finish secondary school. Priština is, for the most part, a Moslem town, and we did not feel totally at home there. So we set off again and settled in Svetozarevo [a small city in Serbia], where I found work in a bank. There I met my husband, who was also from a village. He had left home during the war to serve in the Partisans. After the war he remained in the army and was able to retire a few years after I met him. We remained in Svetozarevo for about 10 years but found life there monotonous. My husband is wild about soccer, so we moved to Belgrade where he could see more games.

My native village of Donji Bunibrod is very close to the city of Leskovac. I came from a poor peasant family and was the third of six children. I managed to finish four grades of elementary school but could not continue because of our poverty. In 1953 I was drafted into the army and served near the city of Subotica in Vojvodina. While there it became clear to me that I could have a better life than in the village. After my military service I returned home and married the daughter of our neighbor. Our two children were born in the village. We had only 1.5 hectares of land and it was of poor quality. I made up my mind that there was no alternative other than coming to the city. My mother and father did not want me to go and they still urge me to return home. I went directly to Belgrade. My wife and children remained in the village for about a year until I was able to get established. I would advise others to do the same. I have just helped my brother come here to live. In a big city a good worker won't stay unemployed.

I was born in a village near Ohrid in Macedonia. It is a small place with about 100 people. Though some parts of the land are fairly fertile, much of it is stony. The people work hard but live poorly. I come from a very large family, with seven sisters and brothers who are all still in the village. After I finished elementary school I decided to leave. There was not enough land to support us all. First I went to Skopje [the capital of the Macedonian Republic], *where I worked part time as an unskilled laborer and studied at nights to become an accountant. I remained there for a few years and then made up my mind to continue on to Belgrade. Belgrade is bigger, with more jobs and better facilities for study.*

I am from the village of Semedraž near Gornji Milanovac. I am the youngest of two brothers and three sisters. I lived in the village until I was 23 except for the time I spent in the army. I was a peasant: I plowed, reaped, and herded animals, what every other man in the village did. In the village I was able to finish six grades of elementary school, and in the army was able to continue studying. It was there that I began to see that the world was larger than the village. When I returned home from my service, I felt a new capability, that I could succeed in obtaining a higher education, and I felt it would be a shame and a waste to stay on the land. My sister, Gordana, was already in Belgrade, working as a bookbinder. Also, my mother's brother and his wife lived in Belgrade. I felt secure having kin in the city who would offer me a place to live. I think I was bored in the village. There the houses were dispersed and we lived apart. It was always the same amusements and the same people!

I was born in Macedonia in a village near Kriva Palanka. We lived very poorly because the land was not fertile and holdings were small. After the war we were given land which was confiscated from the švabi [Volksdeutsch] *in Vojvodina. I met my husband there. He had come with his family from Montenegro, and they too had received a parcel of rich land. Three years ago we were married, and shortly afterward my husband suggested that we could make a still better living in Belgrade. So we decided to give it a try. We are not very far from our families, and if things don't work out we can always go home. However, so far I can't complain, and in fact, we have brought my sister to live with us so she can get a better education.*

I am from the village of Miloševac near Šamac in Bosnia. I was the younger of two brothers. When I was only 4 years old, my father died of typhus and our family was left with 4.5 hectares of good land. We are lucky that our village is located on the plains near the Sava River. In spite of this, it was very difficult after my father's death. My mother worked the land alone with a little help from her brothers. She worked hard, but what else could she do? My brother and I pitched in as much as we could, but we were only children. I remember how poor we were. When I was 18 I got a job as a construction laborer in Modriča, 7 kilometers away. It wasn't a very good job but the money I made helped out. I worked until I was taken into the army. I served my term in Bihać in Bosnia. After I got out of the army I returned to my village. I went back to work in Modriča and saved some money to repair our house, which was in very bad condition. With the help of friends in the village I got the work done, and then I felt free to leave. The land couldn't produce enough for us all. I knew that my mother and brother, who now had a wife and two children, would get along better without me, and that I could contribute something if I could find a job. I decided to try my luck in Belgrade.

I come from the village of Lipovac, 18 kilometers from Aleksinac in Serbia. I was born in a poor peasant family and had one younger brother. I learned to be a blacksmith in our village. Lipovac has about 130 houses and is in the mountains. We are a strong people but very poor. My father died in 1948 and left my mother a widow. My brother and I had to help her work the land so we could stay alive. We have 3 hectares of poor land; I would say it is fourth-class soil. We raise wheat, corn, and plums—we have more plums than anything else. I remember how poorly we lived; we rarely ate meat. I slept on straw and didn't know that life could be better. During 1957 and 1958 I went into the Air Corps to serve my military obligation. I had never really been far away from my village until then. In the town of Sombor where I was stationed I saw something of another kind of life. I was a good soldier and was promoted several times. When I returned to the village I was disillusioned by the way people lived. I made up my mind to leave because I knew there wasn't enough land for all of us. My brother had gotten married and already had a child, and I wanted to get married too. I knew that if I didn't leave we would all die of starvation on the land. We had never divided the holding, and so when I left, naturally it remained in the hands of my mother and brother. I was apprehensive about going to Belgrade because I had no friends or relatives in the city. I gathered my courage and went straight to the capital, and everything has worked out all right.

I was born in the town of Požarevac but my father comes from the nearby village of Prugovo. My father, who was a doctor, died during the Second World War. After his death, my mother took us three girls to live with her parents in Zaječar. It is a small city with no real educational opportunities so, when I wanted to study law, I came to Belgrade, since my father's sister lives here. I have been in the city for 11 years, living with my aunt and her son. My mother was happy that I could stay with Aunt Milica; she knew I would be protected and she wouldn't have to worry about me going wrong. In Zaječar, life was quiet and peaceful but monotonous, and I wanted to enjoy some of the excitement of the big city.

CHAPTER V

THE NEW URBANITES: ESTABLISHING A BASE IN THE CITY

Introduction

The migrant brings with him to the city many of the behavioral patterns and assumptions associated with rural life. His appearance and mannerisms frequently brand him as a villager. He often arrives without financial resources or guaranteed employment. He is immediately faced with problems of survival, and must quickly find work and shelter. If he has friends, relatives, or contacts with former residents of his village in Belgrade, he is in an advantageous position and can expect some aid in getting settled. If he knows no one in the city, he must fend for himself in an unfamiliar environment, in surroundings which must at times appear incomprehensible and hostile. If he possesses qualifications in a trade, specialized education, or employment experience outside of agriculture, his lot will probably be easier. In this respect, those who migrate from provincial towns generally encounter less difficulties, since they come armed with some knowledge of urban life, and are frequently skilled workers with a history of relevant employment.

However, in spite of the many problems and anxieties he must face as a new resident of Belgrade, the peasant migrant enjoys many advantages that rural peoples in similar situations in other parts of the world do not. For example, unlike the Andean Indian who is drawn to Lima or other Peruvian coastal cities (cf. Hammel, 1969a, pp. 103–106), the Serbian villager in Belgrade finds himself among those who speak the same language and spring from the same historical and cultural tradition. Moreover, most of his urban compatriots trace very recent roots to the countryside, and frequently maintain close bonds with their own rural kin. For example, no urban-born informant with whom I spoke lacked ties with the village, or hesitated to admit contact with peasant kin. In one instance, a physicist related that he usually spent his yearly vacation helping his grandfather with the harvest in a village in western Serbia.[1]

On the whole, Belgradians hold the peasant migrant in reasonably high regard, though they may laugh at his lack of sophistication about urban life, and joke about his village ways. He is most often treated with tolerance, and is frequently held up as a high moral example. Expressions of esteem for the villager are not uncommon among city Serbs:

Our man [the peasant] *is honest and hospitable.*

Our peasant is shrewd and knows how to get along.

The peasants have always supported the nation [Serbia] *. . . our culture comes from them.*

Criticism of the villager is seldom hostile as long as he is a Serb, and negative regional stereotypes are usually couched in the form of humor or good-natured jesting:

*Serbian and Montenegrin peasants are very intelligent because they come from an area of hills and forest, but our **banaćani** [people*

[1] I encountered the young man in question reaping hay during the summer of 1966 in the village of Donja Borina.

from Banat] *live on the plains and their brains are clogged with dust.*

The most valuable thing in the world is a drop of Montenegrin sweat. Look around you, you never see one working hard. [Not a very negative stereotype in a culture with a poorly developed work ethic.]

On the other hand, urbanites for the most part avoid public behavior that would suggest recent peasant origins. Moreover, there is a commonly held belief among city elites that modern rural culture represents a somewhat degenerate version of an earlier "pure" form of Serbian national tradition.

While the overt philosophy of the new Yugoslavia is one of egalitarianism, a general pattern of social stratification can be discerned, one which differentiates between peasants, unskilled and skilled urban workers, and the professional and managerial classes. These distinctions are, however, far less stringent than in, for example, many parts of western Europe,[2] and there is an overriding recognition that all Serbs share a common heritage and recent origins in the peasantry. Moreover, the Communist regime has actively sought village support, and though Marxist ideology foresees no future place in its evolutionary scheme for an independent peasantry (cf. Mitrany, 1951), its ethical basis tends to validate an equality of opportunity for all individuals.

Belgrade is sometimes described as "a big village," and this is essentially a recognition of the many similarities between rural and urban Serbian culture, a fact that tends to reduce the severity of problems faced by the peasant migrant in the city. Even so, the change from rural to urban residence is a mixed blessing, and acculturation is not immediate, but rather a continuing process sometimes spanning generations.[3] In any case, the abandonment of old ways and the acquiring of a new life style is never easy, and as the Serbian proverb says, "Every beginning is difficult" (*Svaki početak je težak*). Petar's experience is illustrative of this point:

[2]For example, see Banfield (1958), Cornelisen (1970), Levi (1947), and Silone (1961) regarding class structure and interclass relations in southern Italy.

[3]Burić (1968), in a study carried out in the Serbian industrial city of Kragujevac, indicates that the family life of migrants is seldom transformed to contemporary urban standards during the lifetime of the migrating generation, and that important changes take place only within the second generation in the city.

I left the village in 1961 and went directly to Belgrade. I used to wear tight peasant pants at home, but I bought some used city clothes for the trip; I was afraid to look different. I arrived in the city poor as one can be, without friends or relatives to help me. When I first came to Belgrade, I found it strange and did not like it at all. I missed my home and family. I used to think of the pleasant times I had alone in the wooded mountains, but then the thought would come to me of how poor we were and how miserably we lived in the village. So, I persevered.

Housing and Employment

The two most basic problems faced by the migrant in the city are those of housing and employment. Without a permanent job and space for his family, he cannot really be said to have established roots in the city. The mass destruction of the Second World War and the rapid growth of the urban population has created a severe housing shortage in all major Yugoslav cities. One of the principal tenets of the new socialist state is that the government "owes each family an adequate dwelling unit with minimum standards [p. 144]"; however, this objective remains far from realized (Fisher, 1966).[4] The inability of many new residents to find even minimally adequate quarters for their families is undoubtedly one of the most significant factors in the delayed migration of wives and children to join their husbands in Belgrade.

High-rise apartments are a prominent feature of the Belgrade skyline and new construction is evident in all parts of the city. However, building has not kept pace with the demand, and access to contemporary accommodations is not easy. Theoretically, housing may be obtained by impersonal means: through the organs of local government or from the enterprise by which the individual is employed. Larger and more successful firms are in a position to offer their workers more and better-quality housing, while smaller or less prosperous ones may control no living units at all. Workers with scarce skills are likely to be offered modern housing as an inducement to employment, whereas those who lack special qualifications, or are for any other reason in a less competitive position, will probably be unable to initially secure

[4]Regarding housing policy and municipal administration, see Fisher (1966, pp. 113–144).

any guarantee of an apartment or house. Thus, the problems of employment, education, and housing are difficult to examine separately. The unskilled worker with an elementary education or less, and who lacks seniority, is most likely to pay the highest rent for the least desirable housing. Those who depend on impersonal means for acquiring housing may wait for years on lists without success, and the benefits of connections (*veze*) and political activism should not be discounted, although most informants stated that membership in the Communist Party was now far less significant than formerly.

The advantages of housing obtained in the public sector of the economy are enormous. Rents are uniformly low; the quality is, for the most part, high by Yugoslav standards; and the renter is in many cases able to purchase his apartment upon occupancy or after a specific period of tenancy. Those who cannot find housing through the socialist sector must fend for themselves on the private market. Individually owned houses and apartments are available, but most often the rents are so high as to preclude occupancy by all but foreigners and private entrepreneurs. Others must make do in rented rooms, basements, makeshift shacks, or attics. Alternatively, they may live with friends or relatives, or find space outside the city in a nearby village.

In the case of the peasant migrant there is a direct relationship between the length of time in the city and the quality of housing. On the other hand, those from provincial towns and cities generally enter urban society at a higher level, and because of their greater skills and better connections are usually able to acquire contemporary quarters in a shorter length of time. Most migrants show a pattern of spatial mobility within the city, and those who demonstrate occupational mobility are also most liable to move to more adequate housing as part of the process. Thus, the possession of modern living space may be taken as a rough indicator of success in migration.[5]

Belgrade is distinguished from many Western cities by the nature of the geographic distribution of social classes. Though there is some small variation by district, with two principal exceptions there is little correlation between socioeconomic status and locus of residence in Belgrade. The first deviation from the general

[5]Turner (1970) notes the role of housing in urbanizing countries as "a vehicle of social change," and "geographic stability as an agent of social mobility [p. 2]."

pattern is that of Dedinje, which is the undisputed residential locus of the socially elite. This suburb, located among wooded hills near an area of extensive parks and greenery, is the neighborhood inhabited by high government officials, members of the diplomatic corps, some private entrepreneurs, and a few families of more modest means. In spite of its prestigious nature, its villas and gardens seem shabby and ill kept in comparison with similar districts in the West. The second exception is less definitive. There is some tendency for families with origins in the prewar elite and intelligentsia to live just south of the center of the city, within the triangle formed by the Boulevards of Marshall Tito and the Revolution.[6]

Substandard housing also does not show the configurations that are common in much of the West and many other parts of the world. For example, *Funk and Wagnall's Standard College Dictionary* (1963) defines a slum as "a squalid, dirty, overcrowded street or section of a city, marked by poverty and poor living conditions [p. 1265]." This concept of a slum has been formed, to a great extent, by our experience in the United States, where older districts often show a uniform physical deterioration and where concentrations of economically deprived families live. We are also familiar with the situation in Latin America, parts of Western Europe, and Asia, where areas of substandard housing or squatter colonies located on the outskirts of large cities form highly nucleated patterns of settlement characterized by the extreme poverty of the residents. In the case of Belgrade, however, substandard housing shows a fairly even distribution throughout the city, and it would be difficult to categorize one district or area as a slum. In contrast to the pattern in the West, Belgrade slums can be described as "dispersed." Dilapidated wooden barracks converted into family units stand in the shadow of new blocks of modern apartments. Almost hidden from view, an interior courtyard is bordered by deteriorating dwellings of prewar vintage with a single outdoor spigot supplying water for the needs of a dozen families. Others occupy damp cellars with no facilities whatsoever, and their plight remains hidden from public view. Illegal dwellings spring up around Belgrade faster than they can be torn down and replaced by modern housing; however,

[6]Sjoberg (1960, pp. 96–99) describes the pattern of elite residence near the center of the city as one typical of preindustrial urban complexes.

"Dilapidated wooden barracks converted into family units stand in the shadow of new blocks of modern apartments."

they do not take the form of vast nucleated communities. For example, below Kalemegdan Fortress, on the very banks of the Sava and Danube, stand half a dozen or so shanties assembled from every imaginable kind of salvageable material, with roofs of tar paper held in place by heavy stones. Until a few years ago, a plot of land well within the urbanized zone of the city could be bought for as little as 70,000 old dinars (OD) ($56 in United States currency).[7] On such small parcels many have erected makeshift housing, which they gradually improve or simply hold, hoping that contemporary apartments will be built on the spot, since by law, in such cases, the displaced owner must receive both the price of the land and the right to occupancy in the new building with floor space at least equal to his old abode.

The relationship between socioeconomic class, income, and

[7]During 1968, Yugoslavia was in the process of converting its currency from the so-called old dinar (abbreviated OD), with a value of 1250 to the United States dollar, to the "new dinar" with a value of 12.5 to the United States dollar. In this study all values are shown in old dinars.

"Almost hidden from view, an interior courtyard is bordered by deteriorating dwellings of prewar vintage with a single outdoor spigot supplying water for the needs of a dozen families."

housing is far from absolute, though all provide a rough gauge to the level of success in the city. It should be noted, however, that many who are fully employed, well educated, and highly skilled still occupy marginal housing, whereas some virtually unqualified workers may live in modern apartments under very favorable conditions.

The scarcity of housing, the dispersal of slum dwellings throughout the city, and the policy of distributing apartments through local government or socialist enterprises have thus prevented, for the most part, the differentiation of areas within Belgrade according to the socioeconomic level of the inhabitants. For instance, in the apartment house in which I lived during the course of the Belgrade field work, there resided a radio announcer, a retired general, a retired clerk and his wife (who was a charwoman), a semiskilled worker, a municipal judge, a retired journalist, an opera singer, and a policeman. This integration of families of varied backgrounds exerts a positive effect on the acculturation of the rural migrant. Contact by the villager with his immediate urban neighbors familiarizes him with new patterns of behavior at the same time that it exposes the city resident to rural custom and culture.

Although the city shows little internal differentiation by district, individual buildings or complexes often exhibit some occupational or regional characteristics. For example, a housing unit belonging to a construction company will have a high percentage of tenants from south Serbia and Macedonia, since men from these areas have traditionally worked in this field. An army officer with whom I spoke lived in an apartment building which housed only other officers; however, even in such cases there may be a wide range of statuses. For instance, it is not uncommon to find both ordinary workers and the managerial staff of an enterprise living under a single roof.

Not all migrants are able to solve the problem of housing and employment during their first months in the city, and many spend a prolonged period living a precarious existence. Some give up hope and return to their native villages, whereas others persevere and eventually resolve these pressing problems. The case of Djordje, an unmarried 22-year-old, provides an example of a young man who has not yet found solutions to these basic needs, though both his level of skills and educational goals suggest that his story will have a happy ending:

> *I come from a village in Vojvodina but grew up in the town of Aleksinac, where I finished the trade of mechanic. I have been in Belgrade about a year. I really have no job but work at a car wash where the owner lets me pick up odd jobs repairing customers' cars. I have to give him half of whatever I make, and often there is*

no work at all. I don't have enough tools, and things are hard.
I am trying to finish a course at night to become a machinist, and
perhaps that will help me get a better job. I have no home; sometimes
I stay in the shed at work, other times acquaintances will let me
sleep on the floor at their places. Nothing is difficult when you
have no other choice.

A frequent solution for single men arriving in the city is
to obtain communal housing through their employment. A common form is the so-called workers' colony (*radnička kolonija*), of
which there are many in Belgrade. For example, one such colony
I visited belongs to a construction company. It consists of seven
low, yellow-brick buildings with corrugated metal roofs. The complex is reminiscent of a military camp with a barbed-wire fence
enclosing the entire area. There is no attempt at landscaping,
and open spaces between the barracks are allowed to grow rank
with weeds. About 300 men are housed there, with each building
divided into small units holding four or more beds. A separate,
partially open structure contains a latrine and two cold-water
shower outlets. Stevo, who shares quarters with three other peasant
workers, related the following.

I am from a village in Lika [an area in the Dinaric Mountains
of western Croatia] *and have been employed in Belgrade for about*
a year as a semiskilled worker. I am studying at night to become
a construction technician (**gradjevinski tehničar**). *You see, I only*
earn 45,000 OD [$36] *a month, which is just enough for bread.*
With such a poor job I have to live in a dump like this because
it only costs 3,000 OD [$2.40] *a month. For this we get a roof*
over our heads, a bed, a pillow, and three blankets. There is no
place to cook, and I must either eat cold food or take my meals
in a restaurant, which I can't afford. If I can get a better job
maybe I'll find a more pleasant place to live. I can't say this is
any better than the village; there at least I could build a house
and take a wife. Maybe the future will hold something better.

A more satisfactory and comfortable living arrangement for
the migrant alone in Belgrade is a "hotel for bachelors" (*samački*
hotel). Large enterprises maintain dormitories where workers can

live at a reasonable cost. For example, there is a *samački hotel* in the Dorćol District. It is a multistoried building of recent construction with central heating, an adequate number of showers and latrines, and large sleeping-rooms shared by four men. Though there is greater comfort than in a workers' colony, the atmosphere is spartan and institutional, with little or no evident effort at decoration or the creation of an aesthetic environment. Also, there are no facilities for cooking, and the residents must snack on cold foods or take their meals out. The "hotel" is regarded simply as a place to sleep, and keep one's clothes and possessions. Following a common pattern in Serbian society, men do not entertain friends in their living quarters but rather meet them in cafes and restaurants. Moreover, one resident hastened to assure me that "women are not allowed beyond the reception desk because this is where we live, not a whorehouse!" Access to the improved standard of living represented by these accommodations bears some relationship to factors such as seniority in employment and the worker's level of skills. Rade's story illustrates this tendency:

> *I came to Belgrade when I was 15, and have now been here for 11 years. When I first came to the city, I had two acquaintances from a neighboring village who let me stay with them for a few days and loaned me enough money to get by. In those days jobs were easier to find and I was immediately employed by the construction company for which I now work. I started out as an unskilled laborer. The company got me a bed in a **kolonija** in the Karaburma District. I studied at night, finished elementary school, and became a skilled mason. In 1962 I went into the army and served in Montenegro. When I returned, I went back to my old job. I studied for 2 more years at night, and became a master mechanic. When I finished the course and got a better-paying job with my enterprise, I was able to obtain a place in the hotel. It is much better here, and I only pay 4,000 OD [$3.20] a month from my salary of 100,000 OD [$80].*

Perhaps the most advantageous arrangement for the new arrival in Belgrade is, at least initially, to take up residence with relatives. This arrangement not only provides a solution to the problem of housing, but also places the migrant in a familiar context among people who can give support and guidance. The case of Mirjana is an excellent example of how a base was established in the city and how it facilitated the migration to Belgrade of a number of individuals:

> *Mirjana and her husband, Milun, live in an apartment which was built by her brother, who was the first in the family to come to Belgrade. He had gradually brought each of his brothers and sisters from Loznica* [a small industrializing market town in western Serbia] *to live with him and helped them get started in the city. When the brother migrated to Canada, he gave the apartment to Mirjana and Milun. The young couple then invited the husband's brother, Stevo, from Montenegro to reside with them. After Stevo had found a job and moved out, Milun then invited his patrilateral first cousin from Montenegro, Rada, to stay with them while she studied. When Rada secured a job and found other accommodations, Mirjana gave a room to her brother's wife's niece, who had just arrived from Čačak to attend the university.*

Those who lack kin in the city or, for one reason or another, fail to obtain housing through their employment or the state must make do with what they can find. In many cases they will live under conditions inferior to those they had experienced in the village. Though many see no prospects for improvement of their situation and are unhappy, they still remain in Belgrade hoping that somehow life may become better. Others accept their lot more cheerfully and voice optimism regarding the future:

> *We have been married for 3 years but have no children. How can one have children in a single room? We pay 45,000 OD* [$36] *for a room with a kitchen built in one corner. We have no running water or toilet. The walls are always damp. My husband is an unskilled worker and his pay is very low. He attends night school hoping to get a better job. I must work as a waitress so we can get by. I just wish we could get an apartment some day!*

> *I came to Belgrade about a year ago. Though I had finished secondary school, I had a hard time getting a job. I work as a waitress. I make 40,000 OD* [$32] *a month plus food. Recently, my 17-year-old sister came from the village to live with me. She has no job, and*

*we both live on my money. We have a single room with one small
bed and pay 15,000 OD [$12] a month.*

*My sister and I share an apartment with two other families. There
are nine of us in all. My sister and I have a small room to ourselves.
There is a kitchen, a toilet, and two sleeping rooms. One family
sleeps in the living room. We all get along well. I don't mind all
the people, I have always lived like this. I don't like being alone,
I am a very sociable man. Since I have been in the city I have
finished secondary school and risen from an ordinary worker to the
position of chief clerk. I now make 70,000 OD a month [$56],
and my share of the rent is only 1,800 OD [$1.44] a month.
Things are getting better for me all the time.*

Even those who are fortunate enough to obtain family housing
through their places of employment must often be satisfied with
substandard living conditions. Though the quality of housing may
be low, they enjoy greater living space than those who live in
single rooms, and almost always pay substantially lower rents.
For example, Todor and Drina with their two children occupy
quarters in a complex of barracks-like wooden buildings, each
of which has been subdivided into 10 small family apartments.
The "colony" occupies a muddy stretch of untended land rank
with weeds near the banks of the Danube, and belongs to the
construction company for which Todor works as a heavy equipment operator. The family's apartment consists of a single room
and a small kitchen built in an alcove. There is no running water
in this or any of the other living units. There is a cold-water
tap in the courtyard, and a small partially enclosed structure houses
several filthy latrines, the odor from which permeates the entire
area. On occasions the colony is flooded during heavy rains, and
the yard becomes a sea of mud with water standing a foot deep
in places. Health inspectors are said to have ordered the evacuation
of the premises several times, but to no avail. Todor's company
is, however, building new, modern housing across the Danube
in Krnjača, and the family has been promised occupancy there
in about four months. Todor summed up his feelings about the
kolonija:

*I don't enjoy living here, but our luck has been good, and after
New Year's we will move into a new apartment. My income is 70,000*

OD [$56] per month, and our rent is only 2,500 OD [$2]. I worry because it is so hard for my wife; it is difficult for us to keep clean, and she must do the wash in a pan in the corridor. You see and hear everything around here; people drink and beat their wives, and there are always arguments and conflicts with the neighbors. I will be happy to get Drina and the children out of this place.

Settlement in the city is not usually a single event but rather a process of repeated relocation, commencing with the migrant's arrival in Belgrade and often spanning a number of years. Few new arrivals initially find the housing in which they will remain permanently, and the most successful families in the sample experienced considerable spatial mobility within Belgrade before finally achieving a high standard of housing. During this same period of adjustment they also evidenced vertical mobility in terms of education and occupational status. The relationship between occupational mobility and the quality of housing is illustrated by the following narratives.

*I came to Belgrade from my village about 18 years ago. I was lucky and found work immediately as a physical laborer through a friend from home. I had no kin in the city to stay with, so I rented a bed in a barracks. I was frugal and saved my money, and after a number of months I had accumulated a goodly sum which, together with a loan from a friend, enabled me to buy an old wooden shack. I did not purchase the land, just the building. It was a terrible place; there was only a cold-water tap in the yard, the roof leaked, the windows were broken, and in winter the bitter cold winds whipped through the cracks in the walls. But at least it belonged to me and was a start. I worked hard at my job and my employers held me in esteem. I had finished 8 years of elementary school in the village, and had a superficial knowledge of mathematics and bookkeeping. It was for this reason that I was given the position of a clerk (**službenik**). After I had worked about 6 months in my new capacity, my boss arranged for me to move into an apartment controlled by our firm. It was not very comfortable and had no hot water, but it seemed like paradise after what we had gone through. After I had worked for 3 more years, we were given a better apartment* *in New Belgrade. The following year we managed to trade this one for a somewhat larger apartment in Belgrade through the intervention of my concern. However, the building was old and was torn down to be replaced by a factory. This was a stroke of good fortune, since by law they were required to relocate my family in quarters of equal floor space. No such housing was available, so we were awarded two modern apartments. Though this was technically illegal, we got around the difficulty by registering one in my name and the other in that of my minor son. We are doing very well now. I am retired with a pension, my wife works, and we rent out the second apartment to foreigners at far above the going rate.*

I came to the city without my wife and children. I found a job immediately as an unqualified carpenter with the concern for which I still work. I first lived in a workers' colony. This was an uncomfortable and lonely life but I stuck it out. I knew that I could succeed if I worked hard and steadily. I attended night school and became a qualified carpenter. After I had been in the city for about a year, my wife and children came and joined me. We could find no place to live in Belgrade, so we took room and board with some peasants in a village just outside the city. We stayed there for about 2 years, but I found the commuting to work difficult, even though it was just a few kilometers by bus. Also, it was not comfortable in such primitive circumstances. So we moved into the center of Belgrade, renting a single room from a family for the four of us. In the meanwhile I had received a scholarship from my company for further technical training, and was able to become a skilled carpenter and a foreman. Moreover, in 1964 I was invited to become a member of the Communist Party. I considered it an honor and accepted. Our living circumstances improved after this. First, my firm gave us two rooms in a barracks near a construction site where we stayed for 2 years. Then, we had a real piece of luck. I will never forget September 1967; that is the date when we moved into this modern apartment. We have everything: a bedroom, a living room, a large kitchen, a bath, and plenty of water!

Perhaps the significance of adequate housing in the transformation of the peasant to urbanite is best summarized by an informant who stated

Our contemporary apartment is a very important thing for us. With this apartment I began my life as a cultured man.

One cannot overestimate the importance of employment as a determinant of the manner in which the migrant establishes himself in the city. However, the newcomer's ability to find work and to experience occupational mobility is determined to a great extent by fluctuations in the national economy. Hammel (1969b) in discussing success in migration among Yugoslavs, points out that "though some have forged ahead of their peers by virtue of skill or connections. . .the population as a whole has responded to impersonal external constraints [p. 91]." Moreover, though the Serbian economy is still expanding, urbanization in Belgrade has proceeded considerably more rapidly than industrialization, especially during the last few years. However, the majority of respondents in my sample arrived in the capital during periods of accelerated economic expansion, and most take pride in the fact that they were easily able to find employment "without help." The case of Lazar, who came to Belgrade in 1961, is typical of such responses:

I am proud of the fact that I found a job the first day in the city, and received no help from anyone.

Recently, jobs have become more difficult to obtain, a situation reflected in the numbers of unemployed new arrivals who regularly congregate near several of the principal open markets, hoping to secure odd jobs or other casual work. Under such conditions, the importance of connections (*veze*) in finding employment cannot be discounted in a society where personalism normally plays a major role in the functioning of all institutions. With a tightening of the labor market, personal ties have become increasingly more significant. These are especially helpful in cases where one lacks skills in high demand. The following are typical comments on this problem.

*I came to Belgrade in 1948, and in those days it was easy to get a job without help. I found work right away in a cafeteria. Now it is hard to obtain employment without acquaintances (**poznanstvo**).*

I'm disillusioned with what has happened in our country. Only those with relatives or friends in good positions get decent jobs.

Though there is a clear preference for self-help, migrants freely turn to the traditional reciprocal obligations inherent in the institutions of kinship and friendship when conditions make such action advantageous. In this respect, families with established urban contacts will be in a superior position to continue sending members to the city in times of decelerated economic growth. Similarly, it will be shown in the following chapter that urbanites who are able to maintain close ties with the village are provided with a possible avenue of withdrawal in case of economic depression or personal failure in Belgrade.

CHAPTER VI

KINSHIP AND RURAL-URBAN RECIPROCITY

Introduction

Upon his arrival in the city, the rural migrant begins almost at once to develop new networks of exchange within the urban environment. This is both the expression of a conscious process and the inevitable result and by-product of his participation in city life. However, ties to his former home are rarely totally abandoned, and strong viable relationships with the countryside are frequently maintained. In this chapter I will examine the manner in which the traditional corporate kinship structure has adapted to the more individualistic demands of an industrializing nation with a geographically increasingly mobile population. I propose to approach this question both from the standpoint of theoretical models dealing with changes in kinship function and in the light of specific case histories.

While organs of government and other formal impersonal institutions have gradually replaced a number of the functions of kinship in the Yugoslav village during the last century, the strength and significance of traditional relationships should not be underestimated. Though the size and scope of corporate kinship groups have narrowed, much of the associated behavior and ideology has remained. Not only is extrafamilial kinship still a distinctive characteristic of Yugoslav social organization, but in response to changing conditions it has taken on new meanings in a number of areas in which it was previously inoperative. For example, increased spatial mobility has created new needs at the same time that it has placed restrictions on the types of exchange possible.

In a paper dealing with changes in the Croatian kinship system, Barić (1967a) has pointed out that the decline in the importance of the extended family corporation in rural Yugoslavia does not necessarily signify a diminution of the social significance of kinship, but rather simply a reorientation in response to new exigencies. She distinguishes two levels of organization: one is the grouping of certain categories of kin into corporate units, while the second is composed of the substratum of recognized kin that exists in every society outside the conjugal family. With the decline of the *zadruga*, the substratum of kinship organization, which encompasses not only agnatic links but also matrilateral and affinal kin, has emerged as the most significant systematic feature. Thus, what was previously a recessive level of the system has now become its dominant aspect. Barić suggests that this can be best analyzed in terms of ego-centered sets of cognatic or affinal kin providing channels for activities governed by reciprocal rights and obligations. She points out that kinship contains both an ascriptive and an achieved component. The *zadruga*, for instance, can be viewed as an institution in which ascription plays the major role. However, the less dominant the component of ascription, the more important will be that of achievement. Thus, outside the sphere of traditional corporate obligations, the element of personal choice will play a significant role in kinship exchange (cf. Bott, 1957, p. 221), and constant revalidation will be a salient feature of such relationships.

Commenting on Barić's scheme, which distinguishes the infrastructure of a general bilateral network of kinship ties from the superstructure of highly selective links which constitute corporate groups, Hammel (1969d, pp. 188–189) suggests a refinement of this theory. He proposes that kinship systems can be seen as a potentially limitless grid of relationships on which are drawn a series of culturally determined boundaries that specify the extent to which a particular kind and degree of corporacy and solidarity will apply. These boundaries connect grid points of similar corporacy and solidarity for specific social purposes. The manner in which these boundary lines are drawn will vary cross-culturally and, for example, in a society with a strong agnatic bias they will show a warp along monosexual lines. On the other hand, in a society such as ours, where most kinship functions revolve around the nuclear family, the demarcation lines will lie very close to one another near the center of the network, with a few unimportant lines of ritual corporacy lying more distant from the cluster.

One question not dealt with by Hammel's model is that of the degree of obligatoriness or latitude of personal selectivity inherent in specific kinship ties as related to specific social purposes. In other words, a culture will place greater emphasis oh certain obligations and relationships than on others. For example, though there will be some cases where appropriate behavior will be considered obligatory, in others the intensity of expectations will vary. In terms of Hammel's schematic representation, the fields formed by the connecting of grid points could, through the addition of shading, also specify the intensity of associated expectations. Thus, if black were to correspond to an unequivocally morally binding contract, we would expect that a diagram of eighteenth-century Serbian society would exhibit a preponderance of extensive dark areas, if in fact traditional South Slav culture conformed to its descriptions in the ethnographic literature. Conversely, shades of grey would become increasingly evident, with the darkest areas falling ever closer to the point of initial reference, as one progressed through time to the present. What is thus indicated is simply a greater latitude of personal selectivity and breadth of application rather than a sharp decline in the significance of kinship as a social mechanism.

While kinship has generally been regarded as more significant in preindustrial than in contemporary societies, there is increasing evidence that it can play a salient role in the modernization of traditional peoples. For instance, Friedl (1959) describes kinship as a medium for the transmission of national culture to the Greek countryside. Similarly, Lewis (1952) cites continuing ties between migrants in Mexico City and village relatives in Tepoztlán as a factor contributing to their smooth integration into urban life. To perhaps an even greater degree than is the case in either Greece or Mexico, kinship in Yugoslavia can be regarded as a major factor in urbanization and as a medium for social mobility. In this regard, Barić (1967a) finds that in Croatia long-time urban residents and migrants alike tend to view the maintenance of rural kinship ties as advantageous, and that property in the village frequently serves as a focus for family unity. In socialist Yugoslavia, capital investment has been difficult, and land and farm economy provide urbanites a means of extending family holdings. Rural property also provides a place of rest and recreation for the town dweller. In return, the villager can profit from lines of communication and exchange with the city. Barić also notes that within the city, housing and other advantages are frequently obtained through kinship ties whose rights and obligations often override political and economic differences. Perhaps most significantly, continuing ties of kinship provide a material and psychological buffer against misfortune and failure. Similarly, Hammel (1969d, pp. 194–195) underscores the salient role played by kinship in contemporary urban Yugoslavia by pointing to the fact that from a sample of 500 Belgrade industrial workers, a fifth had found employment through the help of a relative, and as late as 1965 over half of another sample of 350 rural-born Serbian workers spent their yearly vacation in the village of their birth.

With the recognition that kinship continues to function as a major medium of social interaction and exchange in Yugoslavia, a number of questions can be posed of the Belgrade field data. Does the migrant continue to regard himself as an extension of the rural household, or does he see himself rather as a separate and independent entity newly established in the city? What advantages are gained, or perceived to be gained, in continuing rural–urban reciprocity? What variables act as a stimulant to continuing close ties and exchange with the village, and what factors adversely affect these relationships? Do ties to the hinterland die out within the migrating generation, or persist among those born in the city? What are the types, frequency and intensity of exchange? How closely do lines of reciprocity follow traditional patterns, and to what degree are they idiosyncratic?

Patterns of Rural–Urban Reciprocity

Ties to the countryside are seldom single purposed; they are rather, to draw on the terminology of Wolf, *manystranded*.[1] Land, however, acts as the single most cohesive element in rural–urban kinship relations. Thus, reciprocity, directly or indirectly, centers most frequently about joint interests in agricultural holdings. Moreover, it is difficult to regard kinship and land tenure separately, since where there are kin in the village there is almost always land as well. By way of contrast, attachment to the rural community itself is relatively weak, and where one no longer has relatives or property in the village, ties are liable to be severed.

Although many migrants retain legal title to property in the village, the folk system operates somewhat independently of official codes regarding inheritance and land tenure. Kin, most frequently brothers, often hold property jointly after the death of the former title holder, and may postpone division of the patrimony indefinitely. Informants who replied that they had "given" the land to a brother, uncle, or other kin when they migrated to Belgrade in no way meant to indicate that they had relinquished title or claim to the holdings; rather, they had simply handed over the effective control and working of the land in their absence. Even the actual transfer of legal rights does not automatically signify an end to cooperation in terms of the land and its produce. Thus, the legal status of the holding or the absence of a member of the household or family group does not bear a necessary relation to corporate rights and obligations. Land tenure still reflects much of the ideology associated with family corporacy, and individualism is the secondary feature, though it asserts itself in a person's idiosyncratic prerogative to choose to abstain from participation

---

[1]See Wolf (1966, pp. 84–85) for a discussion of "manystranded coalitions" in peasant society.

in the system and to search for other avenues of action perceived to be more advantageous.

Though in most cases cooperation and exchange, especially where property is concerned, follow traditional lines of agnatic lineage organization, affinal and uterine links may be exploited where they are found to be more advantageous, or where there has been some disruption of positive affectual relationships with patrilateral kin. The individual exercises his personal prerogative regarding which relationships will be exploited but, as will be seen, the rules governing reciprocity are quite firm and follow fairly rigid patterns.

Though attitudes regarding legal ownership sometimes appear superficially casual, rights to the land are a subject of great emotionality. While some voiced the intention of "never returning to the village to live," most of those who had interest in rural property expressed an intense attachment to the land, and a resolve to never part with their patrimony. In some cases, they regarded village holdings as an inheritance for their children, who indeed were already familiar with the locus of their rural origins.

Land and other property (houses, equipment, livestock, etc.) are often retained in the village when there are no resident members of the family present to exploit the holdings. In such cases the land is either given to sharecropping (*napolica*—literally, division in half) or rented outright. Sometimes a member of the family will reside on the property for part of the year without actually working the land, so as to fulfill legal requirements regarding the amount of land which can be held by absentee landlords.[2]

While many informants expressed fatalistic attitudes about the future, and regarded life as extremely insecure and unpredictable, those who held rights in rural property or maintained close ties with village kin expressed the idea that these connections with the hinterland acted as insurance against misfortune and as a possible avenue of retreat. Not a few informants stated their intention to return eventually to their native places, and viewed their stay in the city as a temporary expedient. Some continued

---

[2]The maximum amount of land which can be legally held by an absentee landlord is reportedly 3 hectares.

to keep a number of their personal possessions and even furniture in the village. Not only the migrating generation but also those born in the city frequently thought in terms of dual residence and closely identified with their parents' village. This tendency was reinforced if both parents came from the same place; and where the mother and father were from separate villages, loyalties often showed a three-way division (to Belgrade and both villages). Dual residence is quite common, especially among those past the prime years of productivity. Aged parents, for example, may spend part of the year with a son in the village and the remainder in the city with another, helping with child care and household chores.

Visiting patterns between rural and urban kin may be quite intense, with almost weekly exchanges, or may be limited to a trip home during the yearly summer vacation (*godišnji odmor*). Perhaps the most common visiting pattern consists of the exchange of children. Urban parents send their sons and daughters to spend the summer with village grandparents or other kin. Children on a "vacation" in the village are fully incorporated into peasant life, and are expected not only to participate in agricultural labor but also to conform to village norms. Teenagers who dance to "beat" music and contemporary rhythms in Belgrade join in the village line dances (*kola*) with equal enthusiasm. Thus, a law student may pasture stock and work in the harvest while sojourning with his rural kin. On the other hand, village children enjoy becoming acquainted with the city while residing with urban relatives during their school holidays. Such exchanges tend to act as a leveling device in the society, reducing the differences between urban and rural culture and acting as channels for the dissemination of new ideas and modes of behavior. Children who spend months, or in some cases even years, away from their parents in no way appear to suffer from feelings of rejection or alienation. They are still in the circle of the family, a family in which there is a high degree of substitutability of members.

In terms of rational economic motivation, rural–urban exchange can be profitable to both segments of the population. For those who remain behind in the village, city kin are a source of cash for taxes and material improvements, the bearers of gifts of manufactured goods, the providers of a place to stay while receiving treatment at a city clinic, and a pipeline for excess members of the household who must seek their fortunes off the land. For the city resident, the village not only provides a free site for rest and recreation, and security against the unforeseen, but also a continuing source of agricultural products in a cash-poor economy. Most urban families spend at least 70% of their net income on food, and at that find it difficult to make ends meet (see Appendix II for a comparison of wages and prices). Urbanites may be seen arriving daily in Belgrade by bus and train, returning from visits with rural kin laden with boxes and sacks filled with eggs, meat, cheese, vegetables, and other farm produce. Conversely, one never visits the village without gifts for the members of the household in which he will stay: candy for the children, shirts for the men, headscarfs for the women, coffee, sugar, and sometimes more expensive contributions, such as television sets or farm equipment.

The following cases have been chosen as instances of what may be regarded as relatively intense expressions of rural–urban reciprocity. These examples conform to traditional patterns of corporacy based on patrilineality and agnatic ties.

> My father and mother live in a village near Mladenovac. We have holdings there and we give out the land for sharecropping (**dajemo zemlju u napolicu**), and we take half of the produce. My father divided the inheritance while still living, and I share it with my three sons, who live with me here in Belgrade. Our kitchen is always full of potatoes and other food from the village, enough to last us all winter. We go back and forth to the village whenever we can. It's a good place for the children in the summer, and I like visiting around with the neighbors, having coffee with this one and that.

> I miss my native place even though my parents are dead. My uncle [**stric**—father's brother] and his children are my family. My uncle is not doing too badly but he is still poor. I go home about three times a year. I took 18 days vacation in October, and spent it working with my uncle on the land. I can't act like a big shot when I'm not (**ne mogu da budem veliki gospodin kad nisam**). When I go to the village, I always take gifts, and I also send them money to pay the taxes. When I return to Belgrade from a visit, I bring all the food I want. The land belongs to my brothers and me, as

well as to my uncle. I will never sell my share, and when I can save enough money I will build a nice house there and return every year for my vacation.

My firm recently built a glass factory in Czechoslovakia, and I was able to work there at a much higher salary. I saved a good deal of money, and my trip helped my family in the village because I was able to send them 500,000 OD [$400] *to finish the house. I thought about buying my mother a television set but she is old, and people would come from all around to watch it, and she would have no peace. I look at my work in the city as a cooperation with the people at home. I go home four or five times a year. Why shouldn't I? I like to see my family and the place where my ancestors were born. I am going home next on the 29th of November* [Day of the Republic]. *My brother and his wife have visited me a number of times in Belgrade, but the trip is too hard for my mother. Half of the land belongs to my brother, and we hold it together. I will never sell my part, and I don't want to see the property divided. I think it would be perfectly natural to return to the village to live in my old age. This is where my strongest sentiments lie.*

I visit my village as often as possible. When I go home I stay with my father and married brother. I also try to visit the rest of my kin. I never write, but just arrive when it suits me. Our village is not far from Belgrade, and relatives often visit me here. When I go home I take a present for every member of the household and also for two married sisters and their families. In return, I am given food and drink to bring back to Belgrade. We have not divided the land, and have no plan to do so. When I receive my inheritance I will turn over my share to whomever in the family needs to work it. I will never sell it, God forbid, the land is for my children.

*I left the village when I was only 3 years old, but I still have roots there. My three grandparents are there. I have visited Rosići all my life. During the last 3 years, even though it is far away, I have been six or seven times. People from the village are always coming by our place. This year alone we have had a lot of guests: my mother's brother (**ujak**), my father's sister (**tetka**), two of his brothers (**stričevi**), and two of our sons-in-law* [husbands of the informant's father's brother's daughters—**zetovi**]. *My mother and father go very often to the village. My father gives his mother* *and brothers money, and my parents always return from Rosići with* **rakija** [spirits], **kajmak** [clotted milk], *and sometimes even a pig.*

Evidence that the migrant often remains part of the rural corporate group and regards himself, at least partially, as an urban extension of the village household is strengthened by activities and ideology surrounding the *krsna slava*, a Saint's Day cocelebrated by those who recognize patrilineal descent from a common eponymic ancestor. Commemoration usually takes the form of religious observances and feasting in each *independent* household. Thus, if brothers have divided their patrimony and maintain separate residences, each will hold a festival on the day of their common clan saint. The following examples suggest that many migrants, at least initially, do not regard the city as their actual (spiritual) locus of residence, and still identify strongly with the rural household. However, none of the informants cited have been in Belgrade over eight years, and those in the sample with longer residence did not report similar behavior. The case materials, though limited, suggest that perhaps 10 years of domicile in Belgrade is generally the maximum length of time necessary for the immigrant to identify solidly with his new locus of residence.

> *I won't celebrate our* slava *here in Belgrade as long as my father is alive. We sons will take over when he dies. There must be one* slava *while there is one estate (**mora biti jedna slava dok je jedno imanje**). I don't have my own icon, but we keep our image of St. Steven (**Sveti Stefan**) at home in the village.*

> *I don't celebrate the **slava** but my mother and brother in the village do it for me.*

> *My mother and brother celebrate our **slava** of St. John (**Sveti Jovan**) for me in the village. I don't have much idea about religion and I leave it up to them.*

> *I am a member of the Party and don't have much use for religion. I don't celebrate our **slava**, but my father does. When he dies, my older brother in the village will probably take it over for us.*

Even among recent migrants there appears to be some individual variation as to whether a separate celebration will be held. In the case of one family, for example, a festive meal is prepared on the occasion of the *slava* though they consider the most important observance to be that in the village. This somewhat abridged commemoration has been their custom since migration. It should be noted that, although the Yugoslav government does not carry on overt persecution of religion, there still exist some subtle pressures, usually through one's employment, which might act as deterrents to open religious observances in the city. Given the tradition of ritual corporacy, it may be convenient to let one's village kin, who are in effect independent peasant entrepreneurs or subsistence farmers, carry out family religious obligations.

While corporacy in the traditional Serbian village was based on the patrilocally extended household, cooperation between uterine kin and affines was not uncommon. Such reciprocity was, however, often limited by distance, since patterns of residence were patrilocal, and agnatic exogamy was strictly observed. Residence in the city, on the other hand, frequently places a married couple equidistant from both the wife's and husband's kin. While women almost never retain interest in land, they nevertheless may develop intense patterns of reciprocity with their families. The following case provides an example where exchange is carried on with both the husband's and wife's village kin.

> *We do not always spend our vacations in the same place. This year we went to my husband's village in Kordun* [Croatia]. *We stayed with his brother, the one to whom he gave the land. The door is always open to us, and we take what we want* [agricultural produce]. *Sometimes we go to my relatives in Šodolovci in Slavonia* [Croatia], *and it's the same with them. They give us cheese, wine, and meat, and we take them gifts in return.*

In cases where reciprocity with the husband's kin is perceived to be unproductive, or some event had disrupted positive affectual relationships, exchange may be shifted partially or entirely to the wife's family. The following is an illustration where ties have been severed with the informant's patrilateral relations due to unfulfilled economic expectations. The informant's feelings about this underscore the strong moral imperatives inherent in kinship relationships:

> *I was born in the village, but only because my mother and father were visiting my father's family at the time. Actually, our residence was in Belgrade. When I was young I stayed with my father's people in the village every summer. It was pleasant there and I enjoyed life in the country. Well, that has all come to an end. The last time I was there was 10 years ago. My uncles, my father's three brothers, behaved very badly, and I can never forget it or understand how they could betray us when we needed them most. After my father died, they knew we were in terrible financial condition but all they did was try to take our share of the inheritance. This is why my closest contacts are with my mother's family. My mother has a* **miraz** [inheritance or dowry in land given when there are no inheriting sons] *of 3 hectares. My mother received her* **miraz** *when she was married. It was 7 hectares, but according to the present law she can only keep 3 if she does not live on the land. She has turned her property over to the village collective to work for her in return for a yearly rent. I travel two or three times a year to my mother's village to see after the holding. The land is our only savings and security.*

The case of Čedo, an 18-year-old student, provides a striking example of intense reciprocity with matrilateral kin. Čedo's preference for his mother's lineage can be explained principally in the light of his alienation from his father and a strong, but not atypical, attachment to his mother. Moreover, the father does not have a large, cohesive kinship group into which the conjugal family could be incorporated.

> *My mother was born in the village of Drenovac, near Šabac. Her father was the richest peasant in the village, but he died in 1947 and this changed my mother's life. Her parents were patriarchal and everyone did what the father said without question. My grandmother was left with four children, and this was not easy. My father's sister was a teacher in the village, and my father met my mother through her. He was 16 years older than my mother, and she did not want to marry him but she was used to obeying. When my grandmother told her to go with him, my mother did so. I don't*

think my parents have ever been happy together. My mother was young and wanted to have some pleasure in life, but my father would not allow it. My mother works and takes care of the house. My father never stays home, he goes out every night. He is a **vradalama** [an unpredictable person]; *he doesn't treat us right. I absolutely like my mother better than my father, and my brother feels the same way. I spend the summers with my mother's brother (* **ujak** *) in the village. It is a very nice place. My mother's lineage (* **familija**³ *) has eight households (* **kuće** *) in the village. My mother's kin cooperate a great deal. This is the way they get along, and they help us get along too. When I stay with my uncle I never pay anything, but I work with the rest of them. I always take presents when I go to the village; something for everyone in the household as well as a gift for my mother's sister (* **tetka** *), who lives in a village nearby. We send all of our old clothes to my mother's family, and save our schoolbooks for the village children. When I return to Belgrade I bring cheese, beans, and preserves. Every year my uncle kills a hog for us, and the meat lasts all winter. My uncle's children visit us every year during the New Year's vacation. He has three sons, and the oldest is 15. They enjoy coming to the city; it gives them status in the village. When I go to Drenovac, all the young people try to get to know me because they think it is something wonderful to live in Belgrade. Last year I went to the village four times. In the summer I went for a change of air, then in the fall I took my uncle's youngest son home after a visit with us. In the winter I went to my uncle's* **slava**, *and in the early spring I picked up the meat which they had smoked for us. People come from the village to visit us too, and they always bring food. My mother's mother spends every winter with us, and does all the cooking and housework. This year she brought onions, potatoes, wheat flour, and cornmeal.*

Only a few informants failed to carry on some sort of reciprocity with kin who lived outside of Belgrade in villages or provincial towns. There were, however, some differences as to the manner in which these relations were maintained. The major contrast in behavior patterns did not separate recent arrivals from those

³In Serbia proper, *familija* means "lineage," corresponding to the Montenegrin usage *bratstvo*, whereas *porodica* is the usual Serbian term for the nuclear family or immediate household. In Montenegro *porodica* is applied to a group of agnatically closely related households (i.e., an intermediate-range lineage).

born in the city, but rather distinguished the working class from intellectuals and professionals. Working-class respondents emphasized economic exchange to a significantly greater extent than did elites. Among those of higher educational and socioeconomic status, material reciprocity tended more often to be of a symbolic rather than a substantive nature. This distinction is not a firm one, and individual choice plays an important role. Moreover, a number of other variables also relate to the nature and strength of rural–urban reciprocity: the distance of kin from Belgrade; the relative isolation or poverty of the rural community; the biological closeness of the kin involved; the quality of the specific interpersonal relations as determined by individual and family histories.

The following provides an example of a type of reciprocity which is essentially symbolic, ritualistic, and nonmaterial in its emphasis. Sava is an intellectual who is well established in Belgrade with a fairly secure financial base. Nevertheless, he holds great affection for his native town, which is, however, at a great distance from the city, isolated in the mountains of Montenegro. Sava's father and stepmother still live in Plav, on a lake of the same name. Once a week his father sends him trout which he catches in the lake during the warm summer months. He gives the fish to a bus driver, who telephones from the station when he arrives. I was visiting the family one day when the call came announcing the arrival of the fish. It was a hot day, and great excitement centered around the fact that the fish might spoil, so I offered to take Sava to the station in my car. When we arrived, the bus driver presented my friend with a newspaper-wrapped package of fish. There then followed a madcap drive around Belgrade during which Sava distributed fish to his kin and affines. One fish went to his wife's brother's wife's brother (*prijatelj*), another to a patrilateral female cousin (*unuka*—father's brother's granddaughter), and several to an old lady of undetermined relationship called *baba Lena* (grandmother Helen), who in return gave Sava 20 kilos of lard. Other forms of reciprocity, in this case, center about yearly visits to Montenegro, the attendance at family crisis rites (weddings, *krsne slave,* plural of *krsna slava*; and funerals), and the exchange of small gifts and favors.

In another instance, the informant belongs to a highly

urbanized intellectual family in which all household members are city-born. The respondent was nevertheless able to supply genealogical information regarding 80 consanguine and affinal kin of whom only 20 were born in Belgrade. Of the total number she personally knew 30:

> *Our family is like many urban families; we have social contacts on an almost equal basis with both kin and friends. I have the closest association with my mother's brothers and their families. One lives in Belgrade and the other in Sarajevo. I also frequently see my maternal grandmother's brother's two children, who both reside in Belgrade. I also visit my paternal grandmother in Ivanjica [a* small town near Užički Požeg] *at least three times a year, and she frequently comes to Belgrade to stay with us. I am very close to her. Small presents must be exchanged on a visit. It would be a shame to go empty-handed.*

The following is a case in which reciprocity with the informant's place of birth is adversely affected by distance and the poverty of his native village. Nevertheless, regular ties are maintained because of the closeness and strong affectual nature of the kinship relationships involved.

> *I still have my father and mother, as well as a brother and two sisters, in our village. Donji Bunibrod is far from Belgrade [in* southern Serbia], *and it costs us a good deal to get there. They are very poor, and we can't expect any help from them. It has been two years since we have been there, but no matter what, we see each other once a year at least. My mother is visiting us now, and is at the moment staying with my brother across the river [the* Danube] *in Krnjača. My father is coming on the 29th of November to join her. One must stick by his own!!*

In a similar manner, Ilija is restricted as to the nature of possible reciprocity with his village because of its distance and poverty. However, a profitable exchange is carried on with his wife's family, who live in a relatively rich agricultural area:

> *My wife's parents live in a village near Bačka Palanka, where they settled after the war as colonists [they were relocated on*

land seized from the Volksdeutsch]. *We visit them often; my wife is going tomorrow with our son to see her mother and father, and I will join them on the weekend. They have prepared preserves (zimnice) for us, and you have no idea how important this is. We spend 60,000 OD [$48] a month on food but it should be more. They come to see us often and always bring cheese and other farm produce. We would starve without them. I visit my village only once a year. It is a question of the expense of the trip. Lipovac is far away and isolated. I usually spend my yearly vacation there. I try to take small presents when I go, and manage to send my mother a few thousand dinars a month. My mother and brother have no income except what they can get from the land. I bring almost nothing home from the village because they are so poor. I just can't ask them for anything. My mother visited us last year. This was a real luxury for her. I, of course, paid for the trip.*

Long residence, or even birth in the city, does not necessarily mean a severance of ties with rural kin. For example, Gordana, who was born in Belgrade (as were her parents), was able to supply a genealogy of 116 consanguine and affinal kin of whom only 49 were born in the capital. Of those shown in the genealogy, she has had face-to-face contact with 76, and of these, 20 are residents of three separate villages. However, she tired before completing the genealogy, and did not include numerous kin with whom she was familiar in the village of Galičnik in Macedonia, where she visits yearly with her paternal grandfather's relatives. If the depth and breadth of genealogical knowledge is any measure of kinship solidarity, generations born or reared in the city show a surprising wealth of information regarding both rural and urban kin. In the case of the Djordjević family, the mother and father, who spent their formative years in the village, were able to supply data regarding 154 and 341 individuals, respectively, while their daughter, who has spent 17 of her 18 years in Belgrade, contributed data regarding 103 persons, of whom 73 were not resident in Belgrade and 16 were deceased. Of this total she reported face-to-face relationships with 79, while her father had similar ties with 103, and her mother with 158.

By way of contrast, those who had, for one reason or another, severed ties with kin or who simply lacked an extensive kinship network, expressed feelings of loneliness and insecurity. The narrative of an attractive university student is typical of the manner in which these sentiments are expressed, though her situation may be regarded as somewhat unusual by Yugoslav standards:

> *Most of my family were killed in the war. We have always been very poor and life has been a constant struggle. This is why my parents have gone off to work in Germany. I did not want to give up my studies, so I decided to remain behind in Belgrade. I live in a cheap rented room by myself. I really have no one but an old grandmother in a village about 100 kilometers south of here. I am alone in the world. I go to school and spend the rest of my time in my room. I never go out with men because I have no kin to protect my interests. I am very unhappy and wish I could join my parents.*

It is interesting to note that the two most obviously emotionally disturbed informants in the sample also contributed the shortest genealogies. Twenty-one-year-old Božidar lives with his widowed mother and has no other kin closer than Bosnia. He was able to supply a genealogy of only 28 individuals, and surprised two of his friends who were present during the interview by his lack of familiarity with even the most common extrafamilial kinship terms. He freely expressed his feelings of isolation, stating: "We have no one to turn to." The second case is that of 17-year-old Radovan, who claimed to have "no kin to speak of," and refused to even try to supply genealogical material:

> *We are more or less alone. Everyone is out for himself, and those who have big families are ahead of the game. My parents are divorced, and I live with my mother's parents. My mother works in a small town near Novi Sad; well, I might as well tell you, she is a singer of folk songs in a cafe* [tantamount to prostitution], *and she comes home only once a week. My father has already gotten rid of his second wife, and has gone off to Australia. So there you are, it leaves me with no one except my grandparents.*

An urban resident of at least three generations on both sides, with few ties to village kin, expressed the importance which many attributed to rural-urban reciprocity:

These migrants have it easy while we real city folk must struggle along on what we can earn. When they run out of money, they just run to the village for food; they eat like kings.

The significance of kinship both among rural migrants and long-time urban families is underscored by the intense feelings of disappointment and disillusionment when kinship obligations are not fulfilled. Moreover, statements regarding positive attitudes of respect and affect for kin and family may be taken as indicators of underlying cultural norms and expectations regardless of their sincerity. In this regard, I noted that conversations about kin and family were frequently punctuated by such remarks as: "I can't think of anyone more admirable than my parents"; "My brother is the God of Gods (*Bog Bogova*)"; "My uncle is a remarkable man"; "Our grandfather was a real hero, and can still stand up to anyone."

The evidence from Belgrade leaves little doubt as to the positive role played by kinship and its associated ideology in the Yugoslav urbanization process. The vitality of traditional values and institutions is amply demonstrated by their ability to accommodate themselves and adopt new functions in response to changing social and economic conditions stressing increased individual mobility. Continuing rural–urban reciprocity not only maintains channels for the exchange of goods and the transmission of ideas, but also acts as a positive mechanism, reducing feelings of isolation and alienation among migrants in the city; at the same time this reciprocity assures the villager of the continuing viability of those customs and relationships upon which he most depends for emotional and economic security.

CHAPTER VII

ACCULTURATION TO URBAN LIFE

Introduction

Residence in the city by necessity alters a number of the basic behavioral patterns of the migrant. Some changes are obligatory and stem from the very nature of urban life, for example, the abandonment of work in agriculture in favor of employment in factory or office, a greater dependence on the cash economy, and daily interaction with individuals who are neither kin nor neighbors. On the other hand, Belgrade offers many alternative courses of action and belief whose acceptance is neither obligatory nor necessarily immediate.

Culture Change

A problem in the analysis of changing life styles of migrants in Belgrade is posed by the fact that Serbian urban working-class

126

culture exhibits many common elements with village practice. Current innovations in the society frequently reach the hinterland almost as rapidly as the city, and the principal cultural differences lie not so much between urban and rural peoples, as between professionals and intellectuals on the one hand, and the working class and peasants on the other. By way of illustration, an informant related that in his enterprise there was a total lack of awareness as to which workers were of village birth, and that the level of education was the principal criterion for the formation of cliques and social groups within the factory. Though this respondent had completed several years of higher education, he retained a solid identification with his class of origin (which was, however, not determined on the basis of his rural birth but rather by factors related to his former occupation as a factory worker.

> *You have to watch out for educated people. They are cunning (*lukavi*)*
> *and love intrigue like women. As for good humor and companionship,*
> *I am with the workers.*

The problem of language is another case in point. The manifestation of a regional accent or dialect appears to place the individual at no particular disadvantage. Mitko and Koče, both of whom are native speakers of Macedonian (though considered a separate literary language, it is mutually intelligible with Serbo-Croatian), speak the Belgrade dialect of Serbo-Croatian with a slight accent; however, they mention that few, if any, Serbs make note of their speech patterns. In another instance, a university-educated informant accentuates the use of his native Montenegrin regionalisms and takes great pride in his proficiency in the western dialect of Serbo-Croatian, which he characterizes as "the purest form of Serbian speech." His wife related the following.

> *My husband and his brother are both very verbal and delight in*
> *pitting their skills against each other in a kind of contest to see*
> *who can use the most extravagant Montenegrin expressions.*

On the other hand, this informant is very conscious of his status as an intellectual and is almost pedantic in his attention to grammatical detail. This underscores the point that the major distinctions in Belgrade in terms of social symbolism are drawn between uneducated and literate speech with geographical variations playing a relatively minor role. Thus, rural migrants are most often placed in a category defined by their lower level of education rather than in one directly related to their peasant origins.

Musical taste provides another example calling attention to the similarity between working-class urban culture and that of the hinterland. Both rural migrants and city-born workers expressed a universal preference for "national music" (*narodna muzika*), a contemporary folk form akin in many ways to country-and-western music in the United States. A slight deviation from this pattern may be observed among those of longer city residence in that they also showed some liking for contemporary popular music and Italian-style romantic ballads. Professionals and intellectuals contrasted sharply in this respect, since they generally shunned current folk songs in favor of jazz, Western-style hits, classics, and revivalistic highly polished forms of national music (the National Folk Ballet, etc.).

"Both rural migrants and city-born workers expressed universal preference for national music." Folk musicians serenade a guest at a Belgrade wedding.

It is significant that the entire Yugoslav society is undergoing a rapid transformation, and urban elites, the proletariat, and the peasantry are experiencing similar changes. However, education, the breadth of personal experience, and the level of sophistication are factors which no doubt bear a direct relationship to one's receptivity to innovation. On the other hand, problems associated with the adjustment and accommodation to new ideas and modes of behavior do not occur exclusively among rural migrants and the working class. The introduction of supermarkets in Belgrade provides an interesting case in point. Urban planners in recent years had come to regard "self-service" as the "contemporary mode of shopping," and favored the idea that open peasant markets should be gradually phased out in Belgrade. However, resistance among all classes to this was so great that attempts to eliminate the popular open markets were eventually abandoned (personal communication from Dr. Olivera Burić). In fact, in one case where a peasant market had been replaced by a supermarket, the terrace in front of the building soon became crowded with stalls where village entrepreneurs continued to sell fresh produce even though the same items were stocked inside.[1] Though professionals reported more frequent use of supermarkets than working-class respondents, all informants without exception expressed preference for the open market. Similarly, all those interviewed evidenced considerable prejudice against processed foods and canned goods, and reported shopping patterns typified by daily purchases in small quantities.[2]

During the progress of this study it became increasingly evident that it would be difficult to sharply contrast the life styles of new urbanites with those of older, more established residents of the city. Many observed differences were simply idiosyncratic,

---

[1]This was the site of the former Jovanova Pijaca, which, before the building of a supermarket and furniture store, was one of the larger open markets in Belgrade. There are twelve other open markets in Belgrade: Kalenićeva Pijaca, Bajlonova Pijaca, Zeleni Venac Pijaca. Stari Djeram Pijaca, Palilula Pijaca, Banovo Brdo Pijaca, Rakovica Pijaca, Dušanovac Pijaca, Senjak Pijaca, Karadjordjeva Pijaca, Karaburma Pijaca, and Cvetkova Pijaca.

[2]Observations made in three Belgrade supermarkets on nine occasions showed that 63 customers made purchases averaging 3.6 items each, with the largest purchase consisting of 9 items.

and it was not possible to effectively appose the two groups in any absolute cultural terms.

This is not to say that there are no perceived differences between city and village standards. Some innovations are adopted by almost all migrants immediately prior to, or upon, their arrival in Belgrade. Perhaps the most obvious is a preference for modern dress. In the city, only the very old and members of some national minorities[3] continue to cling to folk costume or bits and parts thereof.[4] Even the traditional headscarf universally worn by village women has been, for the most part, abandoned in the city. On the other hand, perception of contemporary style often evidences an awkward, bizarre, or incomplete realization. In this respect the peasant migrant resembles the longer-established urban proletariat. Both are more or less dependent on often shoddy locally manufactured goods, which, at best, lack variety. The elite (and especially those who would like to view themselves as elite), feeling a need to set the pace and to remain distinct in terms of style, often turn to goods of foreign manufacture. For example, Sava, who entered Belgrade society in the lower range of the professional class, is extremely concerned with matters of dress, and never sets foot on the street without a white shirt and tie. He shows a strong bias against goods of domestic manufacture, as does his wife, who related the following.

> *We go to Trieste about twice a year to buy clothes and cosmetics. Italian clothing is really not of a better quality than ours, but we want something others don't have, even it if costs us a lot of money. It was the goal in my husband's family that everyone would have a white-collar job. They look down on manual labor, and my husband would be ashamed to dress so people would take him for a worker.*

Another change engendered by urban life relates to the perception and utilization of time. Work in the city has placed the migrant on a regular schedule of alternate production and leisure, and he no longer experiences long periods of inactivity during slack agricultural seasons, as in the village. Most informants

---

[3]For example, Albanian men (*šiptari*) commonly continue to wear a small, white felt skullcap, a symbol of both their Islamic faith and national identity.

[4]Serbian peasants who can frequently be seen in national dress on the Belgrade streets are generally visitors from the countryside, not city residents.

found the predictable allocation of their time a positive feature, and none appeared to have had any difficulty adjusting to this new situation, though it should be noted that Yugoslav requirements of punctuality are not, by American standards, rigid.[5] While some patterns for the use of leisure time appear very similar to those in the village, the greatest contrast is not between the migrant and the urban-born but again between the working and professional classes. Working-class informants generally viewed leisure time as an opportunity to "do nothing": to sit and stare into space; to nap; to stroll the streets; to sit in a cafe and chat with friends; or to watch television and listen to national music on the radio. Though professionals also valued most of these activities highly, they additionally more often attended plays and movies, utilized libraries and museums, participated in sports or voluntary associations, and with greater frequency devoted attention to hobbies, such as stamp collecting. In both groups school attendance constituted an important use of free time, but workers viewed education pragmatically, in terms of increasing their qualifications in respect to their employment, whereas professionals, who also took a utilitarian view of supplemental schooling, additionally saw it as a validation of their superior status and level of "culture."

Migration to the city has brought the peasant fully into the cash economy with a concomitant development of an appetite for consumer goods. Virtually all informants, regardless of their origins or status, expressed a desire for specific manufactured items, with the automobile the most coveted object. This trend, however, is also typical of the rural hinterland, and manufactured goods are now reaching the village in sufficient quantities that such desires are already cultivated by the time most migrants reach the city. It is interesting that the homes of village-born and urban informants show only slight differentiation in terms of decor and furnishings within the limits of similar incomes. For instance, rural migrants exhibit no greater or lesser propensity

---

[5]For example, Serbs are very casual regarding the hour of social engagements. Invitations are usually phrased in general terms: "Come tomorrow" or "Come by to supper this evening." A Belgrade dentist related that she had given up her specialty of orthodonture because parents failed to bring their children regularly to appointments and effective treatment could not be carried out. Serbs appear skeptical, for the most part, of future planning, and more than one characterized his life in terms of "living from day to day."

than long-time Belgrade residents to display items of national handicraft or to engage in traditional folk arts or household economic activities. Variations in this respect appear to be, for the most part, individualistic in their nature and bear little relationship to the length of urbanization. The Danilović and Žitović families provide an illustrative contrast in this respect. Both have been in Belgrade for approximately the same length of time, and come from similar village backgrounds in southern Serbia.

During a visit one evening to the Danilovići, Bosiljka proudly showed me the preserves she had made. Every available free space in their tiny apartment was filled with jars of tomatoes, peppers, and *ajvar* (pepper and eggplant relish) which she had prepared during the fall for winter use. A huge sack of dried onions hung on a hook in the combined living and sleeping room. Against one wall stood a box of apples, and on top of the armoire (*orman*) were two bags of wool from her father's sheep, which she was planning to utilize to make quilts (*jorgani*). When I showed interest in her skills, she produced for display numerous items of embroidery and crocheting which she had executed. With evident pride she pointed to the woven rugs (*ćilimi*) which covered the floor and which she explained were the product of her youth when she was preparing her dowry (*devojačka sprema*). Regarding his wife, who is not employed outside the home, Aleksandar stated: "Our marriage is a cooperation, I work in construction, and she does her share at home. My wife's duty is here; she does everything from the broom to the spoon (*od metle do kašike*)."

Attitudes evidenced by the Životić family are quite opposite in their orientation toward the symbols of traditional Serbian folk culture. In this case, too, the wife is unemployed and is expected to take total charge of the household chores and children. However, she does not engage in any handicrafts, as does Bosiljka, although she stated that "all girls from the village know how to do these things." The Životić apartment is furnished exclusively from the limited selection of contemporary Yugoslav products and is totally devoid of items of national art or folkcraft. Nikola explained this, stating: "We are making a new life here in Belgrade, and no longer care about the old ways."

On the other hand, intellectuals often display items of Serbian handicraft in their homes and even engage in their manufacture.

In such cases, folk arts are associated not so much with rural life as with the national tradition as a whole. Mileva is a retired elementary-school teacher whose deceased husband was a judge. She was born in a village but has spent over 35 years in Belgrade. She regularly devotes her free time to the embroidery of traditional motifs, and even gives prominent display to a photograph of herself in national costume.

No area of life investigated produced a sharp cultural dichotomy related to length of urbanization or place of birth. For example, one might expect a significant variation in the field of religion; however, again there was no clear differentiation between rural migrants and urban-born informants. The significant variables were, rather, level of education, socioeconomic status, and membership in the Communist Party. Moreover, none of these provided an absolute indicator of an individual's or a family's patterns of belief and practice. Working-class respondents showed, on the whole, a greater propensity for religiosity and participation in the rites of the Church than did intellectuals. Similarly, dependence on folk beliefs regarding the origins of disease and curing tended to show a correlation with class affiliation and degree of education rather than with place of birth. Dietary habits provide another example of the similarity of rural and urban tastes. Here the relevant variable was the level of affluence, with all informants indicating a strong preference for Serbian national dishes. Cuisine evidences a tenacious resistance to innovation which can be explained in part by the close connection between ideas related to health and curing, and food.

The popular lore of Belgrade would have one believe that the peasant arriving in the capital is exposed to a bewildering world of marvels which he poorly comprehends and often misconstrues. Stories regarding migrants who wash potatoes in the bidet and the dishes in the toilet are myriad. This stereotype, however, reflects only a partial truth. In reality, many technological innovations are as unfamiliar to the long-time urban resident as to the villager, and new ideas and items of material culture are entering the society at a number of levels simultaneously. For example, the informants, regardless of their socioeconomic position, for the most part failed to perceive the total range of uses of the refrigerator. Shopping continues on a day-to-day basis, with no

attempt to stockpile food ahead in order to reduce the frequency
of time-consuming trips to the market place. Food that is prepared
and not totally used is often kept on a shelf or table rather than
under refrigeration. The refrigerator is frequently little more than
a repository for cold beer and a symbol of modernity. One informant, for instance, keeps the refrigerator in the living room and
unplugs it during the winter "because one only takes cold drinks
in the summer." Similarly, I was told of peasants living in remote
villages without electric current who bought radios and kept them
prominently displayed as prestige items.

For the most part, the fairly narrow gap which initially
separates the rural migrant from the urban proletariat is quickly
closed, with the new Belgradian soon falling into the general
scheme of city social stratification and becoming indistinguishable
from other urbanites. This fact should not be minimized in terms
of its positive functions in the process of modernization and
urbanization in Yugoslavia.

Social Change

Perhaps the most radical change that takes place in the life
of the migrant is the physical separation from the traditional community to which he is bound by strong affectual ties and moral
obligations related to ideas of family and kinship corporacy.
However, continuing reciprocity with village kin serves as both
an economic and psychological cushion while new lines of communication and exchange are developed in the city.

Accommodation to urban life involves the creation of networks of social relationships in the new environment. If the migrant has kinship ties in Belgrade, he will most probably turn first
to this source for aid, the satisfaction of social instincts, and reassur-
ance. I have shown that the establishment of a base in the city
acts as a magnet for future migration from the village, and that
new arrivals frequently depend on relatives for help in settlement. Interaction with urban kin rarely ends at this point,
and cooperation usually continues well after the initial problems
of adjustment have been overcome. Relatives provide a ready-
made framework for reciprocity, and the strong ideological basis
of such ties precludes the degree of insecurity often manifested

regarding friendship. In many cases, interaction with kin is sufficiently intense so as to make unnecessary the formation of extensive extrakinship ties in the city. The case of Silvana, who has been in Belgrade for over 20 years, provides an excellent example of this phenomenon:

> *My husband brought me to live in Belgrade when we got married. Shortly after this, we helped my two sisters and my widowed mother come to the city. A third sister lives in Batajnica not far from Belgrade. We rarely go out unless it is to visit my sisters and mother. I bake a young pig (**prase**) almost every Sunday and my family always comes. My husband and I don't go to cafes, but we buy wine and have it at home. My mother, or one or another of my sisters, is here almost every night. We really don't need other amusements.*

Dušan provides a similar example. Though he has been in Belgrade for over 18 years, the vast majority of his social contacts are with consanguine or affinal kin. When asked to supply a list of recent visitors to his home, he remembered 29, of whom 26 were in some way related to him. Of the 29 guests, nine were from Belgrade, and the rest visitors from his village, that of his wife, or provincial towns in Serbia near their native villages.

Though the preceding cases do not appear to constitute unusual instances, the field data suggest that many migrants rely somewhat more heavily on ties of friendship. This is, of course, especially true where one lacks kin in the city and his village is distant. Other things being equal, friendships are perhaps most easily established on the basis of common ethnic and geographical origin. For example, in Belgrade there are several cafes which provide a focus for the congregation of Montenegrins. During the summer the upper terrace of Kalemegdan Park is the site of spontaneous folk dancing and singing. Balkan dances are performed, for the most part, in lines or circles, which can effectively delineate one group of dancers from another. The participants are thus able to differentiate themselves on the basis of region of origin. Furthermore, these Sunday activities show an ethnic segregation, with Montenegrins and Serbs occupying the upper sections of the Park, and Albanians (*šiptari*) relegated to a lower meadow, where they engage in Turkish wrestling and sit cross-legged in circles on the ground exchanging gossip and stories.

Occupation constitutes another important criterion for the establishment of bonds of friendship, and interacts with considerations of regionalism and ethnicity. The case of Pavle provides an illustration. He is employed in the heavy construction industry, which shows a concentration of workers from his native area of southern Serbia. Through his employment he has been able to make contact with others of similar background:

> *My best friends in Belgrade are those with whom I work. I have regular contact with about a dozen friends who are from my village or nearby places, and are employed with me. We see each other often; usually we drop by for a visit or go to a cafe for wine.*

Many respondents evidence a balanced set of relationships weighted more or less equally between kin and friends. This is especially true of the children of migrants and those of longer urban residence. An illustration of this is the case of 18-year-old Miroslav, who shows the same open enthusiasm for kin as does his father, and expresses pleasure in the frequent contacts he maintains with both city and village relatives. On the other hand, he actively participates in a neighborhood clique, and frequently goes on weekend outings with friends from the trade school he attends.

Behavior patterns and the expectations associated with friendship in many ways closely parallel those typical of kinship relationships, with reciprocity being the prime feature of the institution. Thus, friendship is revalidated and maintained through a system of the mutual exchange of services, favors, and gifts. Though friendship often contains a strong affectual element, and the mutual satisfaction of social instincts is certainly a salient feature, Serbs appear to place the greatest value on its utilitarian aspects. Through friends it is possible to obtain political or economic advantage, a job, or the expedition of a legal matter or a bureaucratic procedure. Many respondents reported regular patterns of money borrowing and lending with specific partners. In other words, friendship is viewed as a medium for mutual gain, and relationships are frequently created with an eye for potential material or social advantage.

Exchanges between friends need not be of the same order, nor should accounts be immediately paid. As Foster (1967b) observed, regarding the nature of reciprocity in the Mexican town of Tzintzuntzan, "a very important functional requirement of the system is that an exact balance between two partners never be struck [p. 219]." Thus, favors may be stockpiled, and a number of small services can eventually be traded for a single large consideration. To "settle accounts" with an eye to immediate and precise repayment could only be interpreted as a desire to terminate the relationship.

An American who had lived for several years in Belgrade made the following observation regarding Serbian behavior in regard to friends.

> *We have quite a few Serbian friends. We find them loyal but very possessive. If we don't see them once or twice a week, they become very upset. They willingly do us favors of all kinds but also never hesitate to ask in return. What is most strange to us is the fact that they want to be our only friends, and when they find out we have others, they tell us terrible tales about them. In America we would consider such lying wrong but they don't. For the Serb, the creation of his imagination becomes reality!*

These observations point out several important characteristics of friendship in Serbia. The intensity of exchange is not a necessary indication of the stability of the institution, but rather suggests a high level of insecurity regarding such relationships. Indeed, friendship lacks the firm moral basis which underlies family and kinship ties. Foster's model of the *image of limited good* (1967b, pp. 122–152) can be applied to the interpretation of Serbian assumptions and behavior in regard to friendship. The responses of informants indicate that there is a general belief that friendship is not only ephemeral but also that it exists in limited quantities. Moreover, friends may be easily alienated, stolen, or subverted, and are seen as competing for scarce material and emotional rewards. The following comments typify the skeptical and cynical attitudes about friendship which I frequently heard expressed.

> *Relationships between people are bad. There are no real friendships. I once had a close girlfriend and we used to study together. There was a test at school one day and I came out better than she. She*

turned on me and accused me of studying secretly. Though I denied it, she never spoke to me again.

Friends, what's that? They are around when they need something, and when you are in trouble they are no place to be found.

When you have a friend people will try and come between you. They will say anything; that you are a thief or a Gypsy, or that your wife is a prostitute. They have no shame!

Such expressions are at variance with the stereotype of Serbian national character, which stresses the warmth of interpersonal relationships and the open-hearted selfless proffering of hospitality. Indeed, much spontaneous behavior would tend to strengthen these generalizations, though the Serbs themselves appear to accept them in the abstract rather than in relation to their own experience and expectations regarding specific interpersonal relationships.

Undoubtedly the need for increased interaction with nonkin in the city is a cause for some insecurity and skepticism on the part of the new migrant.[6] However, the number of social ties one may effectively cultivate and honor are limited, and while one creates new lines of reciprocity, he finds he must also slough off some of his former obligations in the village. In most cases, casual friends and neighbors are the first forgotten unless some subsequent event, such as mutual residence in Belgrade, reactivates the relationship. Moreover, as I have already noted in the previous chapter, one of the adaptations of the traditional kinship system to increased geographical mobility has been a greater prerogative on the part of the individual as to which specific obligations are to be recognized and to what degree. Thus, contacts and exchange with some (usually more distant) kin may be minimalized, or even discontinued, upon settlement in the city.

There remains one relationship to which I have not yet directed attention, that of fictive kinship or ritual sponsorship, *kumstvo*. In many ways *kumstvo* can be viewed as an institution intermediate between friendship and kinship. It is validated by contractual

---

[6]Kinship relationships also engender feelings of insecurity and skepticism, as this Serbian proverb indicates: "If a brother were good, God too would have one" (*Da je brat dobar, i Bog bi ga imao*).

exchange as well as by ritual and moral sanctification, and it exhibits aspects of both achievement and ascription. Sponsors at baptism and marriage, and sometimes ritual first haircutting, are called for by Serbian custom. In the traditional culture, *kumstvo* reflects the corporate nature of familial organization in that ties of ritual sponsorship are generally contracted between households or lineages, rather than individuals. Hammel (1968, p. 9) observes that although Orthodox Canon Law says nothing about succession to ritual statuses, the Serbian folk theory prescribes that the positions of sponsor and sponsored be inherited in the male line, as are other material and ritual possessions. The collective nature of the institution is also reflected in its terminology, with *kum* (godfather) and *kuma* (godmother) applied as reciprocal terms to all males and females except the sponsored children in the two families joined in fictive kinship. However, the practice of *kumstvo* in this form depends, to a great degree, on the generational and spatial continuity of a stable rural community. On the other hand, urban life and industrialization presuppose a relatively high degree of spatial mobility, making the continuance of such mutual bonds difficult. Thus, it is not surprising that rural migrants in Belgrade are considerably less tenacious in maintaining *kumstvo* relationships with the village than they are those of kinship. Though *kumstvo* behavior reveals considerable individual variation, there is a strong tendency to abandon old ties to the village and to form new ones in the city on the basis of mutual interest and other idiosyncratic criteria. For example, Slavica, who has spent most of her life in Belgrade, was baptized by a member of the family that traditionally supplied sponsors to her father's patriline. Her *kum* lives in Takovo, not far from the village in which she was born, and although she visits her rural kin several times a year, she can remember seeing her godfather only once during these sojourns. Similarly, another informant related:

> *My baptismal* **kum** *is a member of the family which traditionally acts as* **kumovi** [plural of **kum**] *to us. I see him about twice a year. He has two daughters in Belgrade, but I never get together with them. When I choose a sponsor for my wedding, it will be from among my friends here in the city whom I would like to so honor. A year and a half ago I was first witness* (**prvi svedok**) *at the civil*

*marriage of a friend with whom I grew up in Belgrade. We play
basketball together and are great comrades. Though it was only a
civil marriage, he still calls me* **kum**.[7]

The function of urban *kumstvo* does not in essence differ
radically from that in the village, though the form and practice
of the institution have changed considerably. Fictive kinship serves
to sanctify what are perceived as mutually advantageous alliances.
In the city these bonds are created more often between individuals,
whereas in the countryside they tend to link entire family groups
and to be perpetuated through several generations. In most cases
the urban migrant is desirous of creating networks of reciprocity
responsive to his new needs and concerns rather than of perpetuat-
ing old bonds between lineages which no longer hold any economic
or social advantage for him. Moreover, in the village all families
share the same basic needs and interests, and the substitutability
of personnel typical of corporate groups and their interaction
in no way inhibits the function of *kumstvo* as a mode of reciprocity.
In the city, however, diverse economic, occupational, and cultural
orientations play a significant role in the determination of social
relationships outside the family. Moreover, the interests of
individual urban family members are diverse, and it is more
difficult to characterize the household as a solidary, homogeneous
entity. The following cases illustrate the importance of shared
experience as a prime consideration in the choice of urban *kumovi*.

My baptismal godfather is **kum** *Pera, who worked with my father
for a number of years. We see him often. My father did not take
a* **kum** *from his hometown (Užice), but wanted to honor a fellow
worker. It is a new* **kumstvo**.

I was baptized in the village but I don't even know who my **kum**
is. Here in Belgrade I have been **kuma**, *that is, second witness,
at the marriages of two friends from work. We are often together,
and when in need one can count on the aid of his* **kumovi**.

My children were not baptized in the church but they do have a
kum. *He is a friend from work. We became close, so we decided*

[7]According to Yugoslav law, only the civil ceremony is required at marriage. However,
terminology associated with *kumstvo* is maintained even outside the religious context. There
is no evidence that sponsorship ties created without religious ritual differ in their tenacity
or functional content.

to become kumovi *(**da se okumimo**). We agreed, and then I asked
him to a festive dinner prepared in his honor. This is a new **kumstvo**.
I was baptized by a priest who is now dead. He has descendants
in the village and my father pays them respect. I have no contact
with them. I live in the city.*

Another case provides an example where *kumovi* were selected
on the basis of a friendship formed in the city and advantages
were perceived in creating a relationship close at hand. However,
the corporate ideology of the institution is reflected by the fact
that the sponsors of the informant's two children are brothers:

*I christened both children and my husband almost divorced me because
of it. He is a member of the Party and called me superstitious.
Mića's **kum** is a friend from Belgrade and Ljiljana's is his brother
from Vojvodina. I did not pick a **kum** from my husband's village
because it is too far away and the godfather couldn't help the children.
Mića's **kum** just returned from England and brought my son shoes
and a nice present for Ljiljana too.*

Kumstvo ties to the village are not always abandoned, and
old relationships may be maintained while new ones are established
in the city. The following is an example of such a situation.

*My family has a **kumstvo** dating from long ago. The last time
I was in the village, my father asked me to take his place and baptize
a child. I had to hurry back to work so couldn't stay. So my brother
baptized the child for us. I wanted to do it because **kumstvo** is
a very human thing. Recently I was asked to be **kum** at the wedding
of a fellow worker. I would like very much to do so.*

In other instances migrants cling tenaciously to traditional
sponsorship relations in the village, though it is somewhat doubtful
that their children reared in Belgrade will continue to do so.
Bora, who maintains very close ties to his village, related the following.

*My children have a **kum** from our old **kumstvo**, the one that
has passed from generation to generation. We didn't baptize our
two children in the church because the priests want too much money.*

*When each child was about 3 months old, we invited the **kum** to the first haircutting (**pozvali smo kuma na strižbu**) and he gave them their names. We visit our **kum**, who lives in a village near ours, every year.*

The process of social integration of the migrant into city life is a gradual one in which old loyalties to his village or native town are little by little replaced by new ties relevant to the urban community in which he now lives and works. The migrant can be conceived as operating in the context of two social fields simultaneously: that of the village on the basis of traditional ties of familial corporacy, and that of the city in terms of a personally selected network of a more individualistic nature and based on a communality of interest. In terms of the village, the bonds of kinship show the highest degree of tenacity, and also emerge as the favored medium within the city for social and economic reciprocity. Relationships with a person's place of origin based on friendship and ritual sponsorship are less stable, and are the most likely ties to be broken. The criteria by which similar relationships are established in the city indicates that a major result of urbanization and social mobility is an increasing development of individualism.

The Values of City and Country

Several closely related questions remain to be posed regarding the migration experience in terms of the actors involved, and their perception of two alternative life styles. How does the migrant view the changes which have radically altered many aspects of his life? What values does he attach to his former mode of living, and how does he contrast the village in opposition to the city? In what manner are feelings of insecurity and ambivalence regarding the new environment expressed?

On the most general level, individual impressions reflected to a considerable extent the migrant's degree of social mobility and level of success as related to occupation, income, and housing. Thus, those who had been most successful in the city also expressed the most positive evaluations of the urban experience. Curiously, they also voiced a relatively higher evaluation of village life than those who had experienced less success. There was, however, a high degree of concurrence among almost all informants regarding stereotypes of village and urban life in spite of a considerable differential in the fulfillment of expectations about the city.

Among the most interesting observations were those contrasting the city with the village or provincial town as opposing social environments. Individual capacity for action independent of communal responsibility, and the anonymity of the city were repeatedly stressed as positive features of the urban environment. To become "master of one's own fate" is a highly regarded expectation of migration. In contrast, informants viewed the highly personalized social controls of the village negatively:

*The worst thing in the village is the fact that talk and gossip (**prepričavanje**) are favored occupations. In the city one can be himself.*

Life is certainly different in Belgrade. People enjoy more privacy and things are not so strict. This is modern and probably better. In Nikšić [a Montenegrin industrial town of about 20,000 inhabitants] *things are not like this. Even when I was a Gymnasium student I was never allowed out at night. I didn't object because I respected my parents and it was part of our way of life. My husband was the first man I was ever alone with. Before we were married my mother found out all about his family. She did not want me to marry someone from outside of Montenegro because she would have been unable to check on the family.*

Social norms are changing in our country, especially in the city, where the trend is toward more individualism. In the village, parents have a big say in marriages, which are often concluded for economic reasons.

*In my home town, my parents knew everything I did. I was never allowed to walk with a boy even in the daytime until I was 18. What I hate most are the lack of privacy and small-town attitudes (**malogradjanština**).*

Our village is probably too strict, but on the other hand, things are too free in Belgrade. My wife's parents and mine were neighbors in the village, but I scarcely dared look at her before we were married. They would have beaten her if they heard that she had spoken to a boy [**momak**—unmarried male past puberty]. *If a young man wants to see a girl it must be in secret, but that isn't easy because everyone is looking out for your business.*

By way of contrast, many of the same informants who praised individualism expressed insecurities related to the lack of external social controls and the essentially impersonal bases by which they often dealt with people in the course of everyday exchanges:

You never know who people are in this city or if you can trust them. They enjoy deceiving (**vole da prevare**).

How can you depend on people you don't know? They can cheat you and there is no one to care. In the city one can get away with anything.

Particular ambivalence and insecurity were evident in the area of sex-role behavior and the choice of a marriage partner. A number of informants had returned to their villages to take brides, and others had married girls from villages near Belgrade rather than from the city itself. The uncertain past of urban women is a concern reflected in the following examples.

Women were created to satisfy men sexually. I have no use for women who won't indulge in sexual relations, it's not made of glass and won't break [**nije od stakla da se razbije**— a reference to the vagina]. *I don't think I'll marry a Belgrade girl. They are not worthy* (**vredne**) *and true* (**verne**).

I'm not married and would like to find a wife but I haven't run across the right type yet. She must be Serbian and probably from the village, well brought up (**dobro vaspitana**) *and able to behave well in every circumstance. City girls are passed around a lot. It's a matter of training. I have a girlfriend now whom I met one day while I was looking in a store window. After I had known her for a while, I asked about her past so I wouldn't be hearing it second-hand from this one and that. It turned out she had been married twice, and as for boyfriends, I stopped counting at 100. Her life is used up and she has no future. That's the way she is and by 40 she'll be just something for the dogs to chase.*

As for girls in Belgrade, you never know what you are getting though there are still many nice ones. In my mother's village the girls are not free as in the city. You could be there for 10 years and never see a couple holding hands or kissing. In any case, they don't dare do so in the open. A girl would lose her reputation if she flirted openly with boys, and then no one would want her. Everyone knows everyone else, and what they are doing. If a girl openly associated with a boy her parents would know about it before she even got home. In Belgrade the girls are too free. I took my grandmother for a walk one evening in Kalemegdan Park and what she saw so upset her that she almost went back to the village. I don't like this either.

The analysis of these and other cases paints a clear picture of the village and city as opposing types of social organization. This difference is especially obvious in regard to the question of social controls, which in the village are manifested by gossip, backbiting, and ostracism, with concomitant loss of social face. The Serbian village can be characterized as an environment where the individual lacks privacy and anonymity; a person is judged not only by his own actions but also by those of his family and kin; reputation and appearances are more important than real behavior; most eventualities solicit a limited repertoire of socially sanctioned responses; and there are relatively few areas where individual inventiveness and spontaneity may be freely expressed. Belgrade can be described as a social setting where a relatively higher level of anonymity is possible; social controls are to a greater extent impersonal, and in many areas of life internal controls must supplant externally imposed sanctions; there is a wider range of possible responses to given situations; and status is more frequently a reflection of individual achievement or failure rather than family or lineage standing.

On the other hand, the Serbs hold a stereotype as old as the classical civilizations of the Mediterranean (cf. Caro Baroja, 1963), one which views the countryside as a salubrious environment and the city as an entity dangerous to body and spirit alike. Insecurity and ambivalence regarding life in Belgrade are frequently given expression in a framework of concern regarding physical well-being and illness:

Village air is clean, the city is dirty and unhealthy.

*Canned goods and foods wrapped in plastic are harmful. I prepare all my food as we did in the village. You are killing yourself the way you eat! For health, fresh cheese (**mladi sir**), tomatoes, cucumbers, and yogurt are best. One must be careful in the city or he will fall ill.*

It is very healthy in the countryside, especially in our region, where the air is pure because we live at the foot of the mountains. The food is fresh and not spoiled as here in Belgrade.

The noise and confusion of the city are bad for the nerves and health.

Food in the village is more healthy. The best time is the fall when the grapes are ripe. Such fruit can't be seen in the cities.

I am drawn there [to the village], *life is healthier than in the city.*

I like our village even though life is hard there. The air and water are good, superior to the city. Village people are honest and sleep with their doors unlocked. The city is not a safe or healthy place.

However, the city is universally acclaimed as a place of variety and stimulation, whereas the village is regarded as a haven of peace and relaxation:

Our village sometimes becomes monotonous. One can rest too much. In truth, I am used to the noise and dynamics of the city. My life is now active and diverse.

*In the city I go out to cafes all the time. I especially like those with national music where I can kick up my heels (**lumpovati**). In the village there is no variety, but one can get a good rest.*

Most informants expressed a strong sentimental attachment to village culture. This was especially notable in the high evaluation given to festive and ceremonial activities. In this respect, it should be observed that Serbs, villager and urbanite alike, are extremely nationalistic, and the origins of Serbian culture spring, for the most part, from the peasantry. The prestige of folk cuture has been further strengthened and validated by the influence of

Yugoslav ethnography, which has stressed rural custom as a national wealth. Respondents were quite uniform in their high regard for village ritual and folkways:

> *Where I was born the people really know how to celebrate. They are very hospitable, you might say they are born hosts (**oni su rodjeni za gostovanje**).*

> *For me life is better in the city, yet I still like many things in the village. What draws a man to the village are the old customs. When we are there we always go to the cemetery on the Days of the Dead (**zadušnice**). It is a big event and everyone goes to feast and drink.*

> *Life is different in the village than in the city. I like the celebrations in Drenovac. You have never seen anything until you attend a wedding there. It goes on for three days or more. They have races with two-wheeled horse-carts, and there is dancing of the **kolo**. And what music! Musicians of the Šabac area are famous. When there is a holiday they know how to do it up right. You see, there they don't have to get up early the next morning to go to work as we do here in Belgrade.*

> *I like it in the village best during the winter, when they have **prelo*** [a kind of spinning bee held in the evenings characterized by singing, joke telling, and gossip; an important event for unmarried girls], **igranke** [dances], *and* **komišanje** [cornhusking bees]. *Of course, in the summer there are the **vašari*** [stock fairs], *which are also fun.*

Though many informants expressed mixed feelings regarding the city and a large number were plagued with problems of money and poor housing, none indicated they planned to return to the village other than in retirement. Even those who had prospered the least in Belgrade and saw life as a continual struggle against the unpredictable, voiced the intention of "sticking it out" in Belgrade. The advantages of regular employment, fixed hours, greater physical comfort (or its promise), and the availability of the resources of a large community (though many still made little use of them) outweighed sentimental bonds to the countryside. Continuing ties to the village have perhaps resolved the problems of ambivalence and split loyalties with the conviction that indeed one can enjoy the best of two worlds.

CHAPTER VIII

CONCLUSIONS

In 1938 Wirth summarized some widely held sociological generalizations concerning urbanization, stressing the disintegration of bonds of kinship and the disappearance of the traditional basis of social solidarity. He presumed that disorganization and maladaptation were the fates awaiting the rural migrant in the city.[1] However, this old stereotype has not been borne out by the evidence from Belgrade, and the relatively smooth integration of masses of peasants into the fabric of Yugoslav urban life tends to support the contention of Lewis (1952) that "urbanization is not a simple, unitary, universally similar process," but rather one that "assumes different forms and meanings, depending upon the prevailing historic, economic, social and cultural conditions

---

[1]A contemporary of Redfield's, he was undoubtedly influenced by the *folk–urban continuum*, and his work was based principally on the study of North American cities.

[p. 40]." It is with these same assumptions that I have approached the problem of interpreting the process of urbanization and modernization in Serbia.

The Yugoslavs from the time of their settlement in the Balkans were to remain peripheral to great civilizations, and subject to almost constant pressures from economically and politically more powerful neighbors. Of particular significance in this regard were the centuries of Turkish domination, which isolated the South Slavs, especially the Serbs and Bulgars, from the mainstream of European life, and inhibited the growth of an indigenous urban society along Western lines. Thus, in Serbia at the beginning of the nineteenth century there was relatively little national culture outside the peasantry and the Church, and the urban elite were essentially non-Slavic. Moreover, the development of a small, rather provincial, middle class and aristocracy, which had commenced during the nineteenth century, was disrupted by the Second World War and the ensuing Communist social and political revolution.

Under socialism, the rapid growth of industry and the bureaucracy made possible the massive migration of peasants to the city, where they entered a society that, in many ways, lacked a clear-cut stratification conforming to culturally defined criteria of class. For example, many of those who assumed positions of great power following the war were immediately, or by birth, from the peasantry (e.g., Tito). The remarkable expansion of the economy, and the complete replacement of the ruling stratum of the nation, made very rapid mobility possible. In this respect, the peasantization of Belgrade has taken place not only among the proletariat but at all levels of society. Furthermore, even remnants of the old intelligentsia and aristocracy did not always lack ties with the peasantry, and shared with other segments of the population a nationalist fervor and a symbolic devotion to Serbian folkways. Thus, the migrant finds in the capital a body of belief and custom in many ways resembling what he has left behind in the village. Furthermore, the city is overwhelmingly homogeneous in terms of its ethnic and linguistic composition, and the peasant migrant need not interact with persons whose basic assumptions and modes of expression differ radically from his own. Finally, the modernization of the society is not simply a question of the transformation of a backward peasantry, but of an entire nation. Innovations have entered the society at all levels, thus reducing the tendency for pronounced differentiation between migrants and long-time urban residents.

In this work I have focused on the problems of urbanization and culture change in terms of the experiences of individual actors as viewed against the background of a specific historical, cultural, and social context. Data gathered from a sample of Belgrade residents have been analyzed from the standpoint of the decision-making process and the hierarchy of priorities related to the consideration of alternative courses of action and belief.

The data have shown that urbanization involves a series of events in the lives of individuals and families. In the migrating generation (or generations) it usually entails a succession of spatial relocations, each with its concomitant cultural and social dimensions. The initial step within a family revolves around the decision of some individual (usually a male) to abandon his place of residence. Motivations are varied, and relate both to general factors external to the migrant, and to the specific life histories and social positions of those involved. In the case of peasant migrants, important variables are those of inheritance and limited land resources, restricted educational and occupational opportunities, the desire for greater participation in national life and the cash economy, dissatisfaction with village norms and social controls, and the greater stimulation, variety, and individualism offered by the city. However, migration to Belgrade does not usually signify total integration into a new social network or the breaking of traditional ties with the migrant's place of origin. On the contrary, strong bonds of familial corporacy continue to link the migrant to his provincial kin. Such ties often persist several or more generations after the initial move has taken place. Thus, transformation of the migrant is initially spatial and economic, rather than cultural and social. Though the principal economic dependence in the city is on earned wages, lines of material reciprocity with the village are of continuing significance in a cash-poor economy. However, a person's ability to profit from a system of rural–urban exchange depends on a number of variables: the proximity of the village, the nature of kinship ties to the countryside, the relative prosperity of the rural community, the affective quality of specific interpersonal relationships, and the level of alienation from village culture and norms. Frequently the migrant views himself as an urban extension of the village family, and ties to his birthplace act as an insurance policy against possible misfortune or failure in the city. Moreover, relationships with rural kin are also validated by visiting patterns, and ritual and symbolic exchange, activities which often persist when economic reciprocity no longer holds any real significance for the participants.

The structure and values of traditional Serbian society have encouraged the maintenance of strong ties between migrants and their rural kin. These bonds linking two major segments of the nation act as lines of communication, leveling social and cultural differences between village and city, and making possible further mobility from the countryside. Moreover, strong national attachments have placed real limitations on the geographic scope of migration, containing it, for the most part, within internal ethnic boundaries. In the case of Belgrade, this fact has further contributed to the cultural homogeneity of the city's population.

Problems of alienation on the part of the migrant are balanced by continuing participation as part of a village-based kinship network, while new ties are gradually created in the urban community. The flexibility of the Serbian kinship system has been demonstrated by its ability to develop new functions outside of the traditional framework of lineage corporacy in response to increasing individual mobility.

Though there is some evidence of dissatisfaction and ambivalence on the part of the informants, the overwhelming impression is not one of maladjustment, social pathology, and the breakdown of family life and traditional values, but rather one of accommodation and determination to persevere and prosper in the city.

While Yugoslav society exhibits sharp internal contrasts, it would be wrong to presume that the contemporary and traditional poles of the society are inimical and mutually antagonistic, or that this opposition poses a major impediment to the development of the nation. On the contrary, the intermediacy of Yugoslav society is one characterized by a constant exchange and communication between the urban and rural sectors of the community, with urbanization creating a social and cultural continuity between village and city.

CHARACTERISTICS OF THE SAMPLE

Informant number[a]	Sex	Age	Most recent occupation[b]	Birthplace[c]	Type of community where born[d]	Approx. number of contacts
1	M	30	P	S	G	3
2	M	35	S	MT	VC	12
3	F	45	U	S	S	5
4	M	40	S	S	S	4
5	M	40	S	S	S	6
6	M	25	S	S	S	6
7	M	25	S	S	S	6
8	F	45	U	S	S	3
9	M	20	ST	S	V	1
10	M	45	P	S	G	1
11	F	45	P	S	G	7
12	F	40	U	S	S	2
13	F	19	ST	S	G	1
14	M	35	P	C	VC	6
15	M	25	S	S	S	2
16	F	65	H	S	G	1
17	F	35	W	S	S	3
18	M	45	P	BH	V	7
19	F	19	W	S	G	5
20	M	45	P	S	VC	6
21	M	45	S	BH	G	1
22	F	45	H	S	VC	1
23	M	45	P	S	G	3
24	F	35	U	S	S	3
25	M	23	ST	S	G	4
26	M	35	S	MT	VC	2
27	F	35	H	MT	V	1
28	M	45	P	S	G	1
29	M	45	P	M	V	8
30	F	40	H	S	S	1
31	F	45	H	S	S	1
32	M	55	P	S	G	1
33	M	55	P	S	G	14
34	M	45	W	S	S	3
35	M	25	U	C	S	1
36	M	18	U	S	S	1
37	M	20	U	BH	S	1
38	M	25	U	M	S	1
39	F	28	P	S	VC	5
40	M	45	P	S	S	7

[a]An asterisk designates part of an in-depth family study.

[b]P, professional; W, white-collar worker; S, skilled worker; U, unskilled worker; H, housewife; ST, student.

[c]S, Serbia; C, Croatia; BH, Bosnia-Herzegovina; M, Macedonia; MT, Montenegro.

[d]S, *selo* (village); VC, *varošica* (small town); V, *varoš* (town); G, *grad* (city).

Informant number[a]	Sex	Age	Most recent occupation[b]	Birthplace[c]	Type of community where born[d]	Approx. number of contacts
41	F	42	W	MT	S	12
42	M	48	P	S	S	10
43	M	65	S	S	VC	1
44	F	18	ST	S	VC	1
45	F	63	U	S	S	1
46	M	28	U	S	S	1
47	M	53	W	S	S	1
48	M	23	S	S	S	3
49	M	33	S	MT	VC	4
50	M	55	P	C	S	1
51	M	26	W	M	S	5
52	F	32	P	S	G	2
53	F	33	U	C	S	6
54	F	28	U	C	S	4
55	F	43	P	S	G	3
56	F	20	ST	S	S	1
57	F	20	ST	S	G	1
58	F	23	U	M	S	4
59	F	54	U	S	S	3
60	M	55	S	S	V	6
61	F	35	W	S	G	3
62	M	24	ST	S	S	4
63	M	40	S	M	S	3
64	F	23	U	S	S	1
65	M	26	U	S	S	1
66	F	65	P	S	G	2
67	F	20	ST	S	G	3
68	F	31	U	S	V	1
69	M	32	U	S	S	3
70	F	38	U	C	S	1
71	F	39	U	C	S	5
72	M	35	W	MT	VC	8
73	F	29	W	BH	S	3
74	M	48	W	BH	VC	2
75*	M	45	W	C	VC	28
76*	F	41	H	S	S	28
77*	M	4	—	C	G	28
78*	M	40	P	C	S	30
79*	F	35	H	C	S	30
80*	M	14	ST	C	S	30

[a] An asterisk designates part of an in-depth family study.

[b] P, professional; W, white-collar worker; S, skilled worker; U, unskilled worker; H, housewife; ST, student.

[c] S, Serbia; C, Croatia; BH, Bosnia-Herzegovina; M, Macedonia; MT, Montenegro.

[d] S, *selo* (village); VC, *varošica* (small town); V, *varoš* (town); G, *grad* (city).

Informant number[a]	Sex	Age	Most recent occupation[b]	Birthplace[c]	Type of community where born[d]	Approx. number of contacts
81*	F	7	ST	C	G	30
82*	M	62	W	S	S	300
83*	F	45	U	S	S	300
84*	M	21	U	S	S	300
85*	M	19	ST	S	S	300
86*	F	18	ST	S	S	300
87*	M	33	P	MT	VC	100
88*	F	28	W	S	V	100
89*	M	45	P	S	G	3
90*	F	40	P	S	G	3
91*	F	13	ST	S	G	3
92*	F	70	H	S	G	3
93*	F	27	U	BH	S	3
94*	F	30	P	S	VC	40
95*	M	28	P	S	VC	3
96*	F	28	ST	S	G	40
97*	F	40	W	S	G	3
98*	M	70	W	S	VC	3
99*	F	60	H	S	G	3
100*	M	32	ST	S	S	50
101*	F	50	H	S	S	20
102*	F	28	W	S	S	20
103*	F	32	W	C	S	10
104*	F	50	H	C	S	3
105*	F	30	W	C	S	3
106*	F	34	—	C	S	3
107*	F	9	ST	S	G	3
108*	F	20	ST	S	V	10
109*	F	19	ST	S	G	10
110*	M	47	U	S	G	2
111*	F	38	U	S	V	1
112*	M	31	W	S	S	10
113*	F	33	S	S	S	2
114*	F	19	ST	S	G	4
115*	M	52	S	S	V	1
116*	F	40	H	S	VC	4
117*	M	39	S	S	S	5
118*	F	32	H	S	S	5
119*	M	10	ST	S	S	5
120*	F	8	ST	S	S	5

[a]An asterisk designates part of an in-depth family study.

[b]P, professional; W, white-collar worker; S, skilled worker; U, unskilled worker; H, housewife; ST, student.

[c]S, Serbia; C, Croatia; BH, Bosnia-Herzegovina; M, Macedonia; MT, Montenegro.

[d]S, *selo* (village); VC, *varošica* (small town); V, *varoš* (town); G, *grad* (city).

Informant number[a]	Sex	Age	Most recent occupation[b]	Birthplace[c]	Type of community where born[d]	Approx. number of contacts
121*	M	45	S	C	S	10
122*	F	44	U	C	S	10
123*	F	15	ST	S	G	10
124*	M	19	ST	S	G	10
125*	M	36	S	S	S	3
126*	F	36	H	S	S	3
127*	F	11	ST	S	S	3
128*	M	8	ST	S	G	3
129*	M	26	S	S	S	4
130*	M	27	U	BH	S	5
131*	M	23	ST	S	G	4
132*	M	52	W	C	S	4
133*	F	44	H	C	VC	4
134*	F	21	W	S	G	4
135*	M	21	W	S	G	3
136*	M	46	U	S	G	2
137*	F	38	S	S	VC	2
138*	M	21	ST	S	G	4
139*	F	42	H	BH	V	2
140*	M	19	ST	S	G	4
141*	M	44	W	S	VC	2
142*	F	38	W	BH	VC	2
143*	M	15	ST	S	G	2
144*	M	25	W	S	S	7
145*	M	53	S	S	S	5
146*	F	47	H	S	S	5
147*	M	32	U	S	S	5
148*	F	29	U	BH	S	5
149*	M	5	—	S	G	5
150*	M	17	ST	S	G	3
151*	M	76	W	S	S	3
152*	F	72	H	S	S	3
153*	M	18	ST	S	G	30
154*	M	56	S	S	G	10
155*	F	41	U	S	S	15
156*	M	20	ST	S	G	1
157*	M	43	P	S	S	3
158*	F	28	P	S	G	7

[a] An asterisk designates part of an in-depth family study.

[b] P, professional; W, white-collar worker; S, skilled worker; U, unskilled worker; H, housewife; ST, student.

[c] S, Serbia; C, Croatia; BH, Bosnia-Herzegovina; M, Macedonia; MT, Montenegro.

[d] S, *selo* (village); VC, *varošica* (small town); V, *varoš* (town); G, *grad* (city).

Summary of the Sample

1. *Ethnic composition (not shown in Table A)*		Unskilled worker	31
		Housewife	18
Serbs and Montenegrins	134	Student	32
Croats	10	Preschool child	3
Macedonians	3		
Gypsies	7	5. *Birthplace*	
Jews	1	Serbia	115
Hungarians	1	Croatia	21
Turks	1	Bosnia-Herzegovina	10
Russians	1	Montenegro	7
		Macedonia	5
2. *Sex*			
Males	82	6. *Type of community where born*	
Females	76	Village	79
		Small town	21
3. *Age*		Town	11
1–9	6	City	47
10–19	18		
20–29	38	7. *Approximate number of contacts with informant*	
30–39	33		
40–49	41	1–3	80
50–59	12	4–6	37
Over 60	10	7–10	17
		11–20	6
4. *Occupation*		21–30	8
Professional	26	31–50	3
White-collar	26	Over 50	7
Skilled worker	22		

A COMPARISON
OF INCOMES AND PRICES

Family Incomes[a]

Number in family	Income in old dinars	Equivalent in dollars
5	350,000	280
2	320,000	256
3	276,000	220
4	255,000	204
2	240,000	192
4	225,000	180
4	205,000	164
5	200,000	160
3	200,000	160
5	195,000	156
3	193,000	154
4	180,000	144
4	179,000	143
3	140,000	112
3	140,000	112
2	135,000	108
4	130,000	104
2	130,000	104
3	125,000	100
4	120,000	96
1	100,000	80
4	70,000	56
1	60,000	48
2	60,000	48
3	60,000	48
1	50,000	40
3	50,000	40

[a]The net monthly incomes are those of families which participated in the in-depth studies and frequently represent the earnings of more than one individual.

Prices

1. *On the Kalenić open market (Kalenićeva Pijaca), October 1968*

1 kilo white cheese	1,600 OD	$1.28
1 kilo beef with bone	1,370 OD	$1.25
1 kilo boneless pork	1,560 OD	$1.25
1 kilo chicken	1,100 OD	$ .88
1 kilo veal with bone	1,500 OD	$1.20
1 kilo boneless veal	2,100 OD	$1.68
1 egg	60 OD	$ .05
1 kilo tomatoes	200 OD	$ .16
1 kilo cauliflower	300 OD	$ .24
1 kilo carrots	150 OD	$ .12
1 kilo pears	280 OD	$ .22
1 kilo sweet peppers	120 OD	$ .10
1 kilo apples	200 OD	$ .16
1 kilo grapes	300 OD	$ .24
1 kilo green beans	200 OD	$ .16
1 kilo onions	180 OD	$ .14
1 kilo bananas	450 OD	$ .36
1 kilo potatoes	100 OD	$ .08
1 small head lettuce	40 OD	$ .03
1 liter milk	150 OD	$ .10

2. *At supermarkets, June 1968*

6-oz can lemon juice, imported	120 OD	$ .10
19-oz can orange juice, imported	320 OD	$ .26
50-gm can instant coffee	600 OD	$ .48
250-gm can instant cocoa	470 OD	$ .38
1 liter vegetable oil	470 OD	$ .38
1 bar face soap	185 OD	$ .15
200-gm can corned beef	280 OD	$ .22
880-gm can peas	340 OD	$ .27
800-gm can beets	390 OD	$ .31
1 kg white rice	460 OD	$ .37
125-gm can chunk tuna	250 OD	$ .18
135-gm can chicken paté	180 OD	$ .14
1 kg yellow cornmeal	150 OD	$ .12
500-gm sugar	160 OD	$ .13
362-gm white cheese	485 OD	$ .39
1 liter strawberry juice	480 OD	$ .36
500 gm strawberry jam	280 OD	$ .22
400 gm prepared mustard	220 OD	$ .18
860-gm can tomato paste	620 OD	$ .50
500 gm detergent	450 OD	$ .36
1 role toilet paper	110 OD	$ .09
100 gm dry salami	500 OD	$ .40
100 gm chocolate bar	180 OD	$ .14

3. *Of clothing, January 1969*[a]

Women's shoes[b]	8,800–21,000 OD	$ 7.04–16.80
Men's suits[b]	50,000–67,000 OD	$40.00–53.60
Sweaters[b]	11,500–14,600 OD	$ 9.20–11.60
Men's wool slacks[b]	13,900–16,600 OD	$11.12–13.28
Men's dress shirts[b]	5,300–7,400 OD	$ 4.24– 5.92
Men's dress shoes[b]	7,800–16,700 OD	$ 6.24–13.36

4. *Of furniture and appliances, January 1969*

Automatic washer[b]	386,000 OD	$308.80
Table-model television[b]	232,000 OD	$185.60
Electric iron[b]	7,500 OD	$ 6.00
Treadle sewing machine, imported	101,000 OD	$ 80.80
Armchair[b]	137,500 OD	$110.00
Footstool[b]	5,300 OD	$ 4.24
Apartment-size refrigerator[b]	120,000 OD	$ 96.00

[a]The general price range as indicated.
[b]Produced in Yugoslavia.

GLOSSARY OF SERBO-CROATIAN TERMS

ajat	a small outbuilding serving as summer sleeping quarters, usually utilized by young married couples; see *vajat*
ajvar	a relish made from oil, garlic, and cooked eggplant or peppers
amam	Turkish bath
baba	grandmother, old woman, aunt (as an honorific)
badem	city wall, rampart
baklava	a type of Middle Eastern pastry
bakšiš	alms, gratuity, bribe
bratstvo	brotherhood, patriline (from *brat*, brother), maximal lineage
cincar	Tsintsar, Thracian (member of an ethnic group reputed to be of Thracian origin—now almost totally assimilated by the Serbs; a former merchant class)
čast	honor (by extension, "social face")

čaršija   market place, bazaar
ćeten-alva   a type of halvah, a Middle Eastern sweet of chopped nuts, sugar, flour, and oil
ćilim   a type of woven wool rug
dimije   broad pantaloons usually of cotton print material worn by Moslem women
dolina   valley, a geographic term referring to fertile rifts in the karst limestone formation typical of the western Balkans
domazet   a husband living in the household of his wife's natal family, an inheriting son-in-law
esnaf   craft guild
familija   in Montenegro: nuclear family, household; in Serbia: maximal lineage, patriline; see *vamilija*
godišnji odmor   yearly vacation
grad   city
han   inn
igranka   dance, usually refers to a village dance or party
jorgan   quilt
junaštvo   heroism (by extension, maleness)
kafedžija   coffeehouse keeper
kajmak   clotted milk
kapija   gate, gateway; refers to both city gates and the small covered gateways typical of Serbian peasant farmyards
kolo   a circle or line dance
kolonija   colony, housing development, housing project
komišanje   cornhusking bee; see *kumišanje*
korzo   promenade (usually refers to the evening promenade); place where the promenade takes place; see *štafeta*
krsna slava   feast of the lineage patron saint (also refers to the celebration of the patron of a church or other institution; see *krsno ime*
krsno ime   see *krsna slava*
krvna osveta   blood revenge, feud
kuća   house, household
kultura   culture; generally has the connotation of "etiquette" or proper behavior
kum   godfather, sponsor
kuma   godmother, sponsor
kumišanje   see *komišanje*
kumovi   plural of *kum*, a reciprocal term referring to members of the sponsoring and sponsored families (except in reference to sponsored children)
kumstvo   godparenthood, ritual sponsorship, fictive kinship

lumpovati	to carouse
malogradjanština	provinciality, small-town attitudes
miraz	land dowry
mladi sir	young cheese, a fresh white cheese rather similar to the Greek *feta*, also called *srpski sir* (Serbian cheese)
momak	unmarried man past puberty
napolica	sharecropping, in halves
narodna muzika	national music; refers to traditional folk songs or contemporary popular folk-style music
opština	commune; the administrative unit under the level of *republika* (republic)
pečalbarstvo	migrant labor
pleme	tribe
polje	field; a geographic term referring to potholes which have filled with soil typical of the karst limestone formations of the western Balkans
porodica	family; in Serbia refers to the nuclear family or household; in Montenegro refers to a middle-range lineage (composed usually of several agnatically related households)
poznanstvo	acquaintances (by extension, a network of influence)
prase	young pig, usual festive Yugoslav dish
predgradje	suburb
prelo	spinning bee
prijatelj	friend, affine
prvi svedok	best man, first witness
rahat-lokum	Turkish delight, a Middle Eastern candy, also called *ratluk*
rakija	refers to any distilled liquor, usually made from fruit
ručak	midday meal; refers to the main meal of the day, usually taken at about one in the afternoon
sabor	church fair
samački hotel	bachelors' hotel
selo	village
slava	celebration; see *krsna slava*
službenik	clerical worker, clerk
srez	a former administrative unit intermediate between the *opština* and the republic (approximate equivalent of the American county)
starešina	elder (usually in the context of the *zadruga*)
stric	uncle (father's brother)
strižba	ritual first haircutting
šiptar	Albanian (usually refers to a member of the Albanian ethnic minority in Yugoslavia)

šljivovica	plum brandy (regarded as the Yugoslav national drink)
štafeta	see *korzo*
švabo	*Volksdeutsch* (member of the German ethnic minority in Eastern Europe)
tanka krv	thin blood (with reference to the uterine line)
tapan	a large skin-covered drum, also called *tupan*
tetka	aunt (mother's or father's sister)
turska kaldrma	Turkish cobblestone (a type of heavy round cobblestone common in Turkish times)
tvrdjava	fortress, citadel (refers to Kalemegdan Fortress in the case of Belgrade)
ujak	mother's brother
vajat	see *ajat*
vamilija	see *familija*
varoš	town
varošica	small town
vašar	fair, (stock fair)
veze	connections, influence
vrdalama	undependable person, unpredictable person
zadruga	joint household, corporate patrilocally extended family
zadušnice	Day of the Dead, commemoration of the dead
zanatlija	craftsman
zimnice	preserves
zurla	a woodwind instrument common to the Balkans and Middle East, also called *zurna*

REFERENCES

Abu-Lughod, J. Migrant adjustment to city life: the Egyptian case. *American Journal of Sociology,* 1961, **47**, 22–32.

Adams, R. McC. *The evolution of urban society.* Chicago: Aldine, 1966.

Anderson, N. Aspects of urbanism and urbanization. In N. Anderson (Ed.), *Urbanism and urbanization.* Leiden: E. J. Brill, 1964. Pp. 1–6.

Anderson, R. T. *Traditional Europe: A study in anthropology and history.* Belmont, California: Wadsworth, 1971.

Andrić, A., Antić, R., Veselinović, R., & Burić-Zamolo, D. *Beograd u XIX veku (Belgrade in the XIX century).* Belgrade: Muzej Grada Beograda, 1967.

Balen, Š., *Pavelić.* Zagreb: Biblioteka Društva Novinara Hrvatske, 1952.

Banfield, E. C. *The moral basis of a backward society.* Chicago: The Free Press, 1958.

Barić, L. Levels of change in Yugoslav kinship. In M. Freedman (Ed.), *Social organization.* London: Cass and Company, 1967.   (a)

Barić, L. Traditional groups and new economic opportunities in rural Yugoslavia. In R. Firth, (Ed.), *Themes in economic anthropology.* London: Association of Social Anthropologists of the Commonwealth, 1967.   (b)

Barjaktarović, M. P. & Pavković, N. Poreklo i kretanje stanovništva Jadra (The origin and movement of the population of Jadar). *Glasnik Etnografskog Muzeja*, 1965, **27**, 17–44.

Barnes, J. A. Class and committees in a Norwegian island parish. *Human Relations*, 1954, **7**, 39–58.

Barnes, J. A. Networks and political process. In M. J. Swartz (Ed.), *Local level politics*. Chicago: Aldine, 1968. Pp. 107–130.

Barth, F. Introduction. In F. Barth (Ed.), *The role of the entrepreneur in social change in northern Norway*. Bergen-Oslo: Norwegian Universities Press. Pp. 5–18.

Bendix, R. *Max Weber: An intellectual portrait*. Garden City, New York: Doubleday, 1962.

Berreman, G. D. *Behind many masks: Ethnography and impression management in a Himalayan village*. Ithaca, New York: Society for Applied Anthropology.

Blumer, H. Society as symbolic interaction. In A. Rose (Ed.), *Human behavior and social processes*. Boston: Houghton Mifflin, 1962. Pp. 179–192.

Bohannan, P. *Social anthropology*. New York: Holt, 1963.

Bonilla, F. Rio's favelas: The rural slum within the city. In W. Mangin (Ed.), *Peasants in cities*. Boston: Houghton Mifflin, 1970. Pp. 1–19.

Bott, E. Urban families: Conjugal roles and social networks. *Human relations*, 1955, **8**, 345–384.

Bott, E. *Family and social network*. London: Tavistock Publications, 1957.

Breese, G. *Urbanization in newly developing countries*. Englewood Cliffs, New Jersey: Prentice-Hall, 1966.

Browning, H. Recent trends in Latin American urbanization. In G. M. Foster (Ed.), *Contemporary Latin American culture*. New York: Selected Academic Readings, 1968. Pp. BOG-1A to BOG 10-A.

Burić, O. Rural migrants in urban family life. Paper presented at the Second World Congress of Rural Sociology, Amsterdam, The Netherlands, August 1968.

Butterworth, D. A study of the urbanization process among Mixtec migrants from Tilaltongo in Mexico City. *América Indígena*, 1962, **22**, 257–274.

Caro Baroja, J. C. The city and the country: Reflections on some ancient commonplaces. In J. Pitt-Rivers (Ed.), *Mediterranean countrymen*. Paris: Mouton, 1963. Pp. 27–40.

Childe, G. *What happened in history*. Baltimore: Penguin Books, 1964.

Cicourel, A. V. *Method and measurement in sociology*. Glencoe, Illinois: Free Press, 1964.

Coon, C. S. *The races of Europe*. New York: Macmillan, 1939.

Coon, C. S. The mountains of giants: A racial and cultural study of the North Albanian mountain Ghegs. Cambridge, Massachusetts: Papers of The Peabody Museum of American Archaeology and Ethnology, 23, 1950.

Cornelisen, A. *Torregreca: Life, death, miracles*. New York: Dell, 1970.

Coser, L. A., and Rosenberg, B. (Eds) *Sociological theory*. New York: Macmillan, 1964.

Cvijić, J. *La péninsule balkanique: Géographie humaine*. Paris: Librairie Armand Colin, 1918.

Cvijić, J. *Balkansko poluostrvo (The Balkan Peninsula)*. Belgrade: Zavod za Izdavanje Udžbenika.

Darby, E. C., Seton-Watson, R. W., Autry, P., Laffan, R. G. D., & Clissold, S. *A short history of Yugoslavia from early times to 1966*. Cambridge: Cambridge Univ., 1966.

Davis, K. The origin and growth of urbanization in the world. *American Journal of Sociology*, 1955, **60**, 429–437.

Denitch, B. S. *Social mobility and industrialization in a Yugoslav town*. Unpublished doctoral dissertation, Department of Anthropology, University of California at Berkeley, 1969.

Derzhavin, H. C. *Slavyane v drevnosti* (The Slavs in antiquity). Moscow: Izdatel'stvo Akademiyi Nauk SSSR, 1946.

Direkcija Državne Statistike u Beogradu. *Prethodni rezultati popisa stanovništva u Kraljevini Srba, Hrvata i Slovenaca 31 januara 1921 godine* (Preliminary results of the population census in the Kingdom of the Serbs, Croats, and Slovenes January 31, 1921). Sarajevo: Državna Štamparija, 1924.

Djilas, M. *Land without justice*. New York: Harcourt, 1958.

Djurdjev, B. *Historija naroda Jugoslavije* (The history of the Yugoslav peoples). Zagreb: Školska Knjiga, 1961.

Djurdjev, B., Grafenauer, B., & Tadić, J. *Historija naroda Jugoslavije* (The history of the Yugoslav peoples). Zagreb: Školska Knjiga, 1959.

Durham, M. E. *Through the lands of the Serb*. London: Edward Arnold, 1904.

Durham, M. E. *High Albania*. London: Edward Arnold, 1909.

Durham, M. E. *Some tribal origins, laws and customs of the Balkans*. London: George Allen and Unwin, 1928.

Durkheim, E. *The division of labor in society*. New York: Free Press, 1964.

Dvornik, F. *The Slavs/ their early history and civilization*. Boston: American Academy of Arts and Sciences, 1956.

Ehrich, R. W. Geographical and chronological patterns in East Central Europe. In R. W. Ehrich (Ed.), *Chronologies in Old World archaeology*. Chicago: Univ. of Chicago Press, 1965. Pp. 403–458.

Erlich V. St. The South Slav patriarchal family. *Sociological Review*, 1940, **32**, 224–241.

Erlich, V. St. *Family in transition*. Princeton, New Jersey: Princeton Univ. Press, 1966.

Evans-Pritchard, E. E. *Essays in social anthropology*. London: Faber and Faber, 1962.

Federativna Narodna Republika Jugoslavija. *Popis stonovništva 1953 (knjiga XI): Starost, pismenost i narodnost*. (Population census 1953 (Vol. XI): Age, literacy and nationality). Belgrade: Savezni Zavod za Statistiku, 1960.

Fisher, J. C. *Yugoslavia–a multinational state*. San Francisco: Chandler, 1966.

Foster, G. M. What is folk culture? *American Anthropologist*, 1953, **55**, 159–173. (a)

Foster, G. M. Cofradía and compadrazgo in Spain and Spanish America. *Southwest Journal of Anthropology*, 1953, **9**, 1–28. (b)

Foster, G. M. The dyadic contract: A model for the social structure of a Mexican peasant village *American Anthropologist,* 1961, **63**, 1173–1192.

Foster, G. M. *Traditional cultures: And the impact of technological change.* New York: Harper and Row, 1962.

Foster, G. M. The dyadic contract in Tzintzuntzan, II: patron–client relationship. *American Anthropologist,* 1963, **65**, 1280–1294.

Foster, G. M. What is a peasant? In J. M. Potter, M. N. Diaz, & G. M. Foster (Eds.), *Peasant society.* Boston: Little, Brown, 1967. Pp. 2–14. (a)

Foster, G. M. *Tzintzuntzan: Mexican peasants in a changing world.* Boston: Little, Brown, 1967. (b)

Frankfort, H. *The birth of civilization in the near east.* Garden City, New York: Doubleday, 1956.

Friedl, E. The role of kinship in the transmission of national culture to rural villages in mainland Greece. *American Anthropologist,* 1959, **61**, 30–38.

Funk and Wagnall's standard college dictionary. New York: Funk and Wagnalls, 1963.

Gavela, B. O najstarijim etničkim aglomeracijama na području Beograda (Concerning the oldest ethnic agglomerations in the region of Belgrade). In Z. Simić-Milovanović (Ed.), *Godišnjak grada Beograda.* Belgrade: Narodni Odbor Grada Beograda, 1958. Pp. 5–18.

Ginsburg, N. S. The great city in Southeast Asia. *American Journal of Sociology,* 1955, **60**, 455–462.

Glyn, D. *The first civilizations: The archaeology of their origins.* New York: Crowell, 1968.

Goffman, E. *The presentation of self in everyday life.* New York: Doubleday, 1959.

Grafenauer, B., Perović, D., & Šidak, J. *Historija naroda Jugoslavije* (The history of the Yugoslav peoples). Zagreb: Školska Knjiga, 1953.

Halpern, J. M. *A Serbian village.* New York: Columbia Univ. Press, 1958.

Halpern, J. M. *The changing village community.* Englewood Cliffs, New Jersey: Prentice Hall, 1967.

Halpern, J. M. & Anderson, M. D. *The zadruga: A century of change.* Proceedings of the First International Balkan Conference, Sofia, 1966.

Halpern, J. M. & Hammel, E. A. Observations on the intellectual history of othnology and other social sciences in Yugoslavia. *Comparative Studies in Society & History,* 1969, **11** (1), 17–26.

Hammel, E. A. Serbo-Croatian kinship terminology. *Kroeber Anthropological Society Papers,* 1964, **16**, 45–75.

Hammel, E. A. Culture as an information system. *Kroeber Anthropological Papers,* 1964, **31**, 83–91.

Hammel, E. A. The Jewish mother in Serbia. In W. G. Lockwood (Ed.), *Essays in Balkan ethnology.* Berkeley, California: Kroeber Anthropological Society Special Publications, 1, 1967. Pp. 55–62.

Hammel, E. A. *Alternate social structures and ritual relations in the Balkans.* Englewood Cliffs, New Jersey: Prentice-Hall, 1968.

Hammel, E. A. *Power in Ica: The structural history of a Peruvian community.* Boston: Little, Brown, 1969. (a)

Hammel, E. A. *The pink yo-yo: Occupational mobility in Belgrade, ca. 1915–1965.* Berkeley: Institute of International Studies Univ. of California, 1969. (b)

Hammel, E. A. The "Balkan" peasant: A view from Serbia. In P. K. Block (Ed.), *Peasants in the modern world.* Univ. of New Mexico Press, 1969. Pp. 75–98. (c)

Hammel, E. A. Economic change, social mobility and kinship in Serbia. *Southwest Journal of Anthropology,* 1969, **25**, 188–197. (d)

Hammel, E. A. *Preliminary notes on the cycle of lineage fission in southern and eastern Yugoslavia.* Unpublished manuscript.

Hasluck, M. *The unwritten law in Albania.* Cambridge: Cambridge Univ. Press, 1954.

Hawkes, J., & Woolley, L. *Prehistory and the beginnings of civilization.* New York: Harper and Row, 1963.

Hoyt, H., Hoffman, G. W., & Neal, F. W. *Yugoslavia and the new communism.* New York: Twentieth Century Fund, 1962.

Ježić, S. *Hrvatska književnost od početka do danas 1100–1941* (Croatian literature from its beginning to today 1100–1941). Zagreb: Naklada A. Velzek, 1944.

Kalić-Mijušković, J. *Beograd u srednjem veku* (Belgrade in the Middle Ages). Belgrade: Srpska Književna Zadruga, 1967.

Kecmanović, I. *Vuk Karadžić.* Zagreb: Srpsko Kulturno-Prosvejetno Društvo, Prosvjeta, 1951.

Kostić, C. *Seljaci industrijski radnici* (Peasants industrial workers). Belgrade: Rad, 1955.

Kostić, C. *Poseljačenje naših gradova* (The peasantization of our cities). *Politika,* December, 1969.

Kraljevina Jugoslavija Opšta Državna Statistika. *Statistički godišnjak 1938–1939* (Statistical yearbook 1938–1939). Belgrade: Državna Štamparija, 1939.

Kukoleča, S. M. *Analiza privrede Jugoslavije pred II svetski Rat* (An analysis of the Yugoslav economy before the Second World War). Belgrade: Ekonomski Institut FNRJ, 1956.

Levi, C. *Christ stopped at Eboli.* New York: Farrar, Straus, 1947.

Lewis, O. Urbanization without breakdown: a case study. *The Scientific Monthly,* 1952, **75**, 31–41.

Lipset, S. M., & Bendix, R. *Social mobility in industrial society.* Berkeley and Los Angeles: Univ. of California Press, 1963.

Mangin, W. Squatter settlements. *Scientific American,* 1967, **217**(4), 21–29.

Mangin, W. (Ed.). *Peasants in cities.* Boston: Houghton Mifflin, 1970. (a)

Mangin, W. Similarities and differences between two types of Peruvian communities. In W. Mangin (Ed.), *Peasants in cities.* Boston: Houghton Mifflin, 1970. Pp. 20–29. (b)

Mangin, W. Tales from the barriadas. In W. Mangin (Ed.), *Peasants in cities.* Boston: Houghton Mifflin, 1970. Pp. 55–61. (c)

Mangin, W. Urbanization case history in Peru. In W. Mangin (Ed.) *Peasants in Cities.* Boston: Houghton Mifflin, 1970. Pp. 47–54. (d)

Marić, R., Dinić, M., Samardžić, R., Nikolić, M. M., & Jovanović, D. *Beograd kroz vekove* (Belgrade through the centuries). Belgrade: Narodni Univerzitet, 1954.

Marković, T. *Prostitucija: Skripta iz socijalne patologije* (Prostitution: a script from social pathology). Zagreb: Sveučilište u Zagrebu, Visoka Defektološka Škola, 1965.

Mead, M. *The changing culture of an Indian tribe.* New York: Columbia Univ. Press, 1932.

Mills, C. W. *The sociological imagination.* New York: Grove Press, 1961.

Mintz, S., & Wolf, E. An analysis of ritual co-parenthood (compadrazgo). *Southwestern Journal of Anthropology,* 1950, **6**, 341–368.

Mitchell, J. C. (Ed.). *Social networks in urban situations.* Manchester: Manchester Univ. Press, 1969.

Mitrany, D. *Marx against the peasant.* Univ. of North Carolina Press, 1951.

Moore, W. E. *The impact of industry.* Englewood Cliffs, New Jersey: Prentice-Hall, 1965.

Mosley, P. E. The peasant family: The zadruga or communal joint-family in the Balkans and its recent evolution. In C. F. Ware (Ed.), *The cultural approach to history.* New York: Columbia Univ. Press, 1940.

Mosley, P. E. Adaptation for survival: The Varžić zadruga. *Slavonic and East European Review,* 1943, **21** (56), 147–173.

Mosley, P. E. The distribution of the zadruga within southeastern Europe. *The Joshua Starr Memorial Volume, Jewish Social Studies,* 1953, **5**, 219–230.

Moss, L. W., & Cappannari, S. C. Patterns of kinship, comparaggio and community in a south Italian village. *Anthropological Quarterly,* 1960, **33**, 24–32.

Myers, P. *The population of Yugoslavia.* Washington, D.C.: Bureau of the Census U.S. Government Printing Office, 1954.

Naval Intelligence Division, Naval Staff, Admiralty. *A handbook of Serbia, Montenegro, Albania and adjacent parts of Greece.* London: His Majesty's Stationary Office, 1920.

Nemanjić, M. *Neke tendencije u nastanku i obnavljanju stvaralačke inteligencije Srbije* (Some tendencies in the growth and regeneration of intellectual creativity in Serbia). Belgrade: Sociološki Pregled, 1964.

Nikić, L. Džamije u Beogradu (Mosques in Belgrade). In Z. Simić-Milovanović (Ed.), *Godišnjak grada Beograda.* Belgrade: Narodni Odbor Grada Beograda, 1958. Pp. 151–206.

Noyes, G. R. The Serbo-Croatian language. In R. J. Kerner (Ed.), *Yugoslavia.* Berkeley and Los Angeles: Univ. of California Press, 1949. Pp. 279–301.   (a)

Noyes, G. R. The literature of the South Slavs. In R. J. Kerner (Ed.), *Yugoslavia.* Berkeley and Los Angeles: Univ. of California Press, 1949. Pp. 302–315. (b)

Noyes, G. R. *The life and adventures of Dimitrije Obradović.* Berkeley and Los Angeles: Univ. of California Press, 1953.

Obradović, D. *Sabrana dela* (collected works). Belgrade: Prosveta, 1961.

Paunović, M. *Beograd večiti grad* (Belgrade eternal city). Belgrade: N. U. Svetozar Marković, 1968.

Perić, O. (Ed.). *Beograd u devetnaestom veku iz dela stranih pisaca* (Belgrade in the nineteenth century from the works of foreign writers). Belgrade: Biblioteka Grada Beograda, 1967.

Peristiany, J. G. (Ed.). *Honor and shame: The values of Mediterranean society.* London: Weidenfeld and Nikolson, 1965.

Peruničić, B. (Ed.). *Beogradski sud 1819–1839* (The Belgrade court 1819–1839). Belgrade: Istorijski Arhiv Beograda, 1964.

Pitt-Rivers, J. (Ed.). *Mediterranean countrymen.* Paris: Mouton, 1963.

Popović, D. *Beograd kroz vekove* (Belgrade through the centuries). Belgrade: Turistička Štampa, 1964.

Potter, J. Introduction: Peasants in the modern world. In J. M. Potter, M. N. Diaz, & G. M. Foster (Eds.), *Peasant society.* Boston: Little, Brown, 1967. Pp. 378–383. (a)

Potter J. From peasants to rural proletarians: social and economic change in rural communist China. In J. M. Potter, M. N. Diaz, & G. M. Foster (Eds.), *Peasant society.* Boston: Little, Brown, 1967. Pp. 407–419. (b)

Redfield, R. *The folk culture of Yucatan.* Chicago: Univ. of Chicago Press, 1941.

Redfield, R. The folk society. *American Journal of Sociology,* 1947, **52**, 293–308.

Redfield, R. *The village that chose progress.* Chicago: Univ. of Chicago Press, 1950.

Redfield, R. *The primitive world and its transformations.* Ithaca, New York: Cornell Univ. Press, 1953.

Redfield, R. The social organization of tradition. *The Far Eastern Quarterly,* 1955, 15(1).

Redfield, R. *The little community.* Chicago: Univ. of Chicago Press, 1956 (a)

Redfield, R. *Peasant society and culture.* Chicago: Univ. of Chicago Press, 1956. (b)

Redfield, R., & Singer, M. B. The cultural role of cities. *Economic Development and Culture Change,* 1954, **3**, 53–73.

Sanders, W. T. & Price, B. J. *Mesoamerica: The evolution of a civilization.* New York: Random House, 1968.

Silone, I. *Fontamare.* New York: Dell, 1961.

Simić, A. The blood feud in Montenegro. In W. G. Lockwood (Ed.), *Essays in Balkan ethnology.* Berkeley, California: Kroeber Anthropological Society Special Publications, 1, 1967. Pp. 83–94.

Simić, A. Management of the male image in Yugoslavia. *Anthropological Quarterly,* 1969, **42**(2), 89–101.

Sirjamaki, J. *The sociology of cities.* New York: Random House, 1964.

Sjoberg, G. *The preindustrial city.* Glencoe, Illinois: Free Press, 1960.

Socijalistička Federativna Republika Jugoslavija. *Popis stanovništva 1961, v. X: Stanovništva i domacinstva u 1948, 1953, i 1961* (Population census 1961, v. X: Populations and households in 1948, 1953, and 1961). Belgrade: Savezni Zavod za Statistiku, 1965 (a)

Socijalistička Federativna Republika Jugoslavija. *Popis stanovništva 1961, v. XIV: Aktivnost i delatnost* (Population census 1961, v. XIV: Activity and Employment). Belgrade: Savezni Zavod za Statistiku, 1965. (b)

Socijalistička Federativna Republika Jugoslavija. *Statistički kalendar Jugoslavije 1969* (Statistical almanac of Yugoslavia 1969). Belgrade: Savezni Zavod za Statistiku, 1969.

Šolajić, D. (Ed.). *Ratna prošlost Beograda* (The military past of Belgrade). Belgrade: Beogradske Novine, 1954.

Stanković, B. *Nečista krv* (Impure blood). Zagreb: Prosvjeta, 1950.

Steinbeck, J. *Travels with Charley: In search of America.* New York: Viking, 1962.

Taylor, G. The geographical scene. In R. J. Kerner (Ed.), *Yugoslavia.* Berkeley and Los Angeles: Univ. of California Press, 1949. Pp. 2–23.

Tomasevich. J. *Peasants, politics, and economic change in Yugoslavia.* Stanford,

California: Stanford Univ. Press, 1955.

Tomasic, D. *Personality and culture in eastern European politics.* New York: George W. Stewart, 1948.

Tönnies, F. *Community and society.* East Lansing, Michigan: Michigan State Univ. Press, 1957.

Tret'yakov, P. N. *Vostochnoslavyanskiye plemena* (The East Slavic tribes). Moscow: Izdatel'stvo Akademiyi Nauk SSSR, 1953.

Trouton, R. *Peasant renaissance in Yugoslavia 1900–1950.* London: Routledge and Kegan Paul, 1952.

Turner, J. Barriers and channels for housing development in modernizing countries. In W. Mangin (Ed.), *Peasants in cities.* Boston: Houghton Mifflin, 1970. Pp. 1–19.

United Nations Economic and Social Council. World survey of urban and rural population growth: Preliminary report by the Secretary-General. E/Cn.9/187 for Population Commission, 13th Session, Item 4 of the Provisional Agenda, 1965.

United Nations Statistical Office. *Demographic yearbook, 1953.* New York: United Nations, 1964.

United Nations Secretariat, Bureau of Social Affairs, in cooperation with International Labor Office, Food and Agricultural Organization, UNESCO, and World Health Organization. *Report on the world social situation including studies of urbanization in underdeveloped areas.* New York: United Nations, 1957.

Van Loon, H. W. *Van Loon's geography: The story of the world.* Garden City, New York: Garden City Publishing, 1940.

Vucinich, W. S. Yugoslavs of the Moslem faith. In R. J. Kerner (Ed.), *Yugoslavia.* Berkeley and Los Angeles: Univ. of California Press, 1949. Pp. 261–275.   (a)

Vucinich, W. S. The Second World War and beyond. In R. J. Kerner (Ed.), *Yugoslavia.* Berkeley and Los Angeles: Univ. of California Press, 1949. Pp. 353–386.   (b)

Ward. B. The nationalized firm in Yugoslavia. *American Economic Association,* 1965, **55**(2), 65–74.

Weber, M. *Die Verhältnisse der Landarbeiter im ostelbischen Deutschland.* Berlin: Ducker & Humbolt, 1892.

West, R. *Black lamb and grey falcon.* New York: Viking, 1968.

Wirth, L. Urbanism as a way of life. *American Journal of Sociology,* 1938, **44**, 1–24.

Wolf, E. R. *Peasants.* Englewood Cliffs, New Jersey: Prentice Hall, 1966.

SUBJECT INDEX

175